T0106118

# Woman, The Myth

# Woman, The Myth

By

# Ashok Kumar Pant

iUniverse, Inc.
New York   Bloomington

# Woman,The Myth

iUniverse books may be ordered through booksellers or by contacting:

iUniverse
1663 Liberty Drive
Bloomington, IN 47403
www.iuniverse.com
1-800-Authors (1-800-288-4677)

ISBN: 978-1-4502-4919-5 (sc)
ISBN: 978-1-4502-4920-1 (ebook)

Printed in the United States of America

iUniverse rev. date: 08/03/2010

I am extremely thankful to my loving wife Rajani for her continuous moral support. I am highly obliged to Gunjan, Manoj and Jeevan(Poison Guru).

अष्टाशीतिसहस्राणि ये प्रजाभीषिरर्षयः । दक्षिणेनार्यम्णः पन्थानं
ते श्मशानानि भेजिरे ।।
अष्टाशीतिसहस्राणि ये प्रजां नेषिरर्षयः । उत्तरेणार्यम्णः पन्थानं
तेऽमृतत्त्वं हि कल्पते ।।

Those eighty eight thousand sages, who gave up their ascetic way of living thereby adopting the marital life for the sake of sensual pleasure and desire of child, occupied southern region or degraded zone at the river belt of funeral ground after death whereas those eighty eight thousand sages, who kept their lusty feelings in control, become the true follower of the theme of righteous track of northern zone or God and got free from the cycle of incarnations by achieving *Moksha*.

# Preface

At the starting of the era, some moral foundations were kept by the ancient most religion Hinduism and even the present society is running over those hypothesis and considerations. Till now from the prehistoric epoch, nothing new is revealed by the human being whose description is not done in the Hindu religious scriptures. There are found such narrations which appear to be rationally unfeasible in contemporary circumstances but this is also true that on those supposed to be practically unattainable inventions described in the religious testimonials, researches are being conducted in developed countries and will be carried out even in the future. The prophecies and assessments done regarding present era, in the very earlier period of human existence, are still found to be authentic. Such depictions can only be seen in the scriptures of Hindu religion.

The opinion of Hindu religion has always been the subject of contradictions and arguments among the followers of other religions and the religious agnostics. The religious panel code kept numerous times more strict obligations on men but a very little part of those was imposed on women. Hence this was an absolute fallacy that Hindu religion did the gender discrimination and kept women in more severe confinement because the actual situation was just reverse of that.

The fundamental objective of such regulations was to flow the society in such a way to ensure the codes of conducts and morals maintained by exactingly preventing the spread of adultery. Whichever rules in the Hindu codes appear to be very stern are just to ensure people not performing physical or spiritual harlotry. Unfortunately even after taking so much precautions, debauchment remained and cultivated like a never ending series while still rules were rigid to chastise people involved in depraved sexual relations. Hence gradually in the duration of hundreds of thousands years in future, adultery took the place of separate category where the people considering sexually forbidden illicit sexual relations to be a symbol of advancement, congregated as all of them were exiled by the rituals. Then in that category, perhaps a brilliant progeny took birth who kept the foundation of a different society. In this society, the fundamentals of Hindu religion were accepted as it were while the remaining part was added by keeping the view of spiritual pretension, sexual depression and sexual coalition with the religion. Hence a new opinion was formed in which a part of the virtuous codes of Hindu religion was taken while the remaining was made by distorting some ritualistic aphorisms of the Hindu scriptures. Perhaps, in future, this society of the followers of a new stream converted in to a religion. Though, on going in depth of the truth of every religion, it is easily seen that the fundamentals are almost common and are for the wellbeing of the humanity.

To prove the religion to be foremost and the paramount, some of other religions accepted the concept of augmenting the population of the followers by moral or immoral sexual adultery, compelling the followers of other religions to get converted, pretending to assist the destitute of other religions by providing financial enticement thereby provoking them to change their religion and false blaming on other religions. The pseudo followers of almost all the religions blemished the chastity, dignity and codes of their religion and never tried to improve themselves because such attempt of self improvement would have ensured the inferiority of their own society or religion.

What Hinduism says regarding women and what kind of regulations are kept to sustain the moral as well as physical purity of women, a little attempt is done to describe that briefly in the following few lines. This is the compilation of the mythologies of Hindu religion which are in-all proved to be truth in the past as well in the present scenario. As the almost description done in the book is a part of Hindu religious sayings and the thoughts of brilliant ancient sages hence it may be considered as a past or a history to make comparative analysis of it with the current level of chastity and morality of women. A part of description done in the book includes the sexual functioning of women and the way they react in such performances as per the views of great philosopher *Vatsyayan*. Almost every religion kept some code of conducts by applying some laws on men and women to ensure virtuousness. In the religion, where the followers took it as captivity to their freedom and denied to follow the strict appearing norms, there took place the utmost moral decline, sexual debauchment and degradation of women and such every kind of depravity was caused by the women only.

By pursuing the sayings of the religion by accepting the codes of conducts, no religion or the followers become conservative or orthodox because the actual sayings of the religions provide moral strength and maintain the civic sense as well as humanity and ensure the family concept by not allowing the birth of cross-breeds. If the followers of religion disregard the codes of moral conducts of their religion to accomplish the pseudo implication of being forward and proving themselves superior in the blind race of nudity then such attempt done by breaking the religious laws only ensures the rapid increment of debauchment in the descendants.

# Index

# Origin of Creation

In Hindu mythology, according to *Smritis*, lord *Brahama* is the originator of the universe. Lord *Vishnu* is the organizer and director of the universe while Lord *Mahesh* is worshiped as the symbol of devastation. It is assumed that the origin of men and women is done by lord *Brahama*. According to *Manu Smriti-*

द्विधा कृत्वाऽऽत्मनो देहमर्धेन पुरुषोऽभवत् । अर्धेन नारी तस्यां स विराजमसृजत्प्रभुः ।।

Lord *Brahama* divided his body into two parts, one part created man and the other created woman and he originated the process of sexual union as a masculine glaring in man. The sexual union aroused as the source of extreme pleasure gifted by God. Though the process of mating was invoked to increase progeny custom and on the basis of that, the physical differences in-between men and women were created but in this process of making differences among men and women, some basic tendencies were bestowed upon both of the genders. According to *Vishnu Puran:-*

अर्धनारीनरवपुः प्रचण्डोऽतिशरीरवान् । विभजात्मानमित्युक्त्वा तं ब्रह्मान्तर्दधे ततः ।।
तथोक्तोऽसौ द्विधा स्त्रीतं पुरुषत्वं तथाऽकरोत् । विभेदपुरुषत्वं च दशधा चैकधा पुनः ।।
सौम्यासौम्यैस्तदा शान्ताऽशान्तैः स्त्रीतं च स प्रभुः । विभेद बहुधाः देवः स्वरुपैरासितैः सितैः ।।

1

*Rudra*, originated from *Brahama* divided himself in to two halves in the form of man and woman, on the direction of *Brahama*. After this the men were granted with eleven qualities while part of woman nature was conferred by decency, cruelty, calmness, quarrel etc thereby differentiating man and woman from each other.

In adverse geographical environment, men used to struggle more because of physically being stronger than women. Men were busy in arranging facilities while women devoted themselves in proper utilization and arrangement. The reason behind was that to earn the living even with no facility and lacking of material etc, one has to do cut- throat labor and only raw food like fruits and vegetables were available. Men could secure themselves and women when they were enough capable to prove themselves to stand with concept of survival of the fittest. In future, only those breeds could survive whose forefathers have struggled with other creatures and worked hard even in the difficult geographical conditions. As men were physically stronger than women, it was there duty to protect them so as to save their coming breeds. Hence women gave patronage to the men finding them as their security. According to *Vrihadaranayak Upanishad*: –

स ह प्रजापतिरीक्षांचक्र हन्तास्मै प्रतिष्ठां कल्पयानीति स स्त्रिय ससृजे ता ँ सृष्टाऽघ उपास्त तस्मात्स्त्रियमघ उपासीत स एतं प्राञ्चं ग्रावाणमात्मन एव समुदपारयत्तेनैनामभ्यसृजत् ।।

In order to materialize the need of patronage for man, lord *Brahama* created woman, prayed her basic form and hence she is worshipped in the present also. Lord *Brahama* bedecked the lady with the qualities that a righteous lady should possess.

According to the views of followers of Jesus Christ, the source of origin of man was different. As per their opinion, man was created from soil of earth and life was invoked in him through his nostrils. It is told that God advised man not to eat the fruits of a particular tree as the fruits of that tree were in fact the knowledge of proper-improper and moral-immoral. The objective of God behind this suggestion to man was to make him living a complication free life and be even unaware from the sins. God warned man that the moment he will eat those fruits, he would get the sense of wrongdoings and thus would not be able to control over him for not committing alluring sins thereby he too would become mortal like animals. To remove the solitude of man, God took out one of his rib while he was sleeping and did the creation of woman. Thus God created woman out of man. The man said,

"This is now bone of my bones,

And flesh of my flesh;

She shall be called woman,

Because she was taken out of man"

In this situation, the extensive desire for attaining sexual pleasure in women was not considered as an awful quality. The first iniquitous attribute aroused in a woman and in future mostly found in all ladies was because she was originated from man hence the moment she becomes a wife of a man, the couple physically contribute to a single entity and meanwhile lady compel his man to get diverted from his liability for his parents.

A snake came to the woman and told her that there was a tree which was having fruits of good qualities and bad qualities. By eating those fruits, conscience arises in a person and he becomes equivalent to God. Snake also told her that the saying of God that by eating those special fruits a person will die was false. From that moment, bad qualities of blasphemy and distrust on God aroused in her. She found those fruits attractive in looking and one day she relished the fruit and the moment she did that, she got the bad qualities of impatience and avarice. She gave that to her man also. From that instant, awful feature of deceitfulness aroused in her. Because of eating those fruits, prudence vanished in both, man and woman and in the woman this became her basic shortfall while as in case of man, it was due to the betrayal done by woman hence such situation in man sustained even in the future due to presence of woman only. Lack of conscience made them feel that they were naked. God called upon man, but he was delayed, because of the lack of prudence due to the presence of woman. He felt his nudity and vetoed himself to confront God. This was the first and most important victory of woman because by her beauty she was able to deflect man from righteous path of obeying God. When God asked man the reason behind eating the fruits which were even prohibited to be plucked from trees for eating purpose, he spoke truth. When God asked women the same question, she told God that she had been betrayed by the snake. God cursed the woman that now she may feel the extreme pain while giving birth to child and the man, whom she would like to make her slave, in the roll of a husband, shall preside over her if he would be having discretion. To the woman, he said:-

I will greatly multiply

Your pain in childbirth,

In pain you will bring forth children;

Yet your desire will be for husband,

And he will rule over you.

God cursed man that as he gave more importance to the words of his woman and took divine guidance as a rumor, therefore whatever he would try to make his family by adjusting with his wicked wife, shall ruin and be mixed in earth after death along with his family because they all were ultimately originated from the soil.

Cursed in the ground because of your;

In toil you will eat of it

All the days of your life.

Both thorns and thistles it shall grow for you;

And you will eat the plants of the field;

By the sweat of your face

You will eat bread,

Till you return to the ground,

Because from it you were taken;

For you are dust,

And to dust you shall return."

According to Hindu religion, when man and woman initially took birth, they were absolutely free from sin. With time their population increased and due of unavailability of the sources or reasons to commit any kind of sin, they all were sent to heaven after death. Thus all men and women were noble and there was no selection criterion to be done among them to find more worthy persons to go to heaven. So the people who were abstinent even in opposite and adverse conditions shall only get the heaven or get the good living form in next incarnation, with this reason creator invoked the source of sin on earth. It is said that the aim to achieve the above was done by invoking moral-immoral qualities in women. Thus the assessment of men became comparatively easier because of the presence of women conferred by moral-immoral persona. In this way, men had to protect their power of conscience while living with women and also have to prohibit themselves in getting influenced by the immoral basic characteristics of women. Ladies too had to make a difference between virtuous and awful and ensure that their virtuous qualities are more dominating. This is mentioned in *Mahabharath* as follows:-

पूर्वसर्गे तु कौन्तेय साध्यो नार्य इहाभवन् ।।
असाध्यस्तु समुत्पन्ना: कृत्या: सर्गात् प्रजापते: ।
ताभ्य: कामान् यथाकामं प्रादाद्धि स पितामह: ।।
ता: कामलुब्धा: प्रमदा: प्रवाधन्ते नरान् सदा ।

At the time of the origin of this world, all women were devotee towards their husbands, virtuous and free of sins. Debauched women also termed as *kritya* were originated because of not differentiating among virtuous and awful qualities invoked by lord *Brahama* in them and preferring awful deeds more in comparison to virtuous deeds due to the indiscretion. Since then, these corrupted ladies became passionate for sexual pleasure and diverted men from their ethical conduct and duties. A woman with immoral activities is always said to be adulterated by her nature because she herself is deflected from the right path and same she does with the young moral ladies and with the men of morals. Again it is mentioned in *Mahabharath* that no one on this earth is more sinful than sexually and morally corrupt ladies. Women who behave like an insane for sexual pleasure or who have

7

uncontrollable passion for love are like burning fire in the form of a pyre for men and are like a dreadful delusion created by monster of illusion. If a sharp knife, poison, terrible huge sized snake, burning fire and other dangerous detrimental elements are kept on one side while a young lady on the other, then comparatively, a young woman can cause more disaster. Again initially all men and women were devoted to God and acquire heaven after death hence lord *Brahama*, for the selection of right person, created *kritya* in the form of women, full of misdeeds, who initially deflect men from right path and after that become the reason of their devastation.

All human have to move on carrying few basic virtuous and awful qualities. This is to be carried off from one generation to other. Civilization came and people were bifurcated in communities. Even after the dissimilarities caused by the division of human in different religions, boundaries of nations, towns, states and continents, their basic tendencies remained the same. Perhaps from the time of the origin of earth, geographical conditions have changed uncountable times but the psychology of human in sequence of development did not alter. Besides the cycle of life and death, destroying of old and birth of new did the end of the existence of ancestors but still there was something which was exactly the same with the alteration. Changes in *Yugas* took place hence *Treta Yug*, *Satyug* and *Drapar Yug* could not remain unaffected by the curse of mortality. Different *Yugas* left the same moral examples for the upcoming *yug,* examples in which the assessment was done of the virtuous-awful ways, nature and behavior of mankind. Forecasting and assumptions done in the extreme early period regarding the *Kaliyug* or the present are found to be truth. Again moral-immoral, truth-false, vice-virtue and proper-improper tendencies of human are found to be same in *Kaliyug* as it were in early *Yugs.* In early *Yugs,* virtues as truth, empathy and conscience superimposed over their antonyms properties while now in the present scenario, virtues are lost and transgressions are found to be dominating over it.

# The Preface of *Kaliyuga*

The preface and depiction of *Kaliyug* was decided earlier to other *Yugs*. At the starting of the era, God himself decided the destiny of his creation. The assumption done about *Kaliyug* numerous centuries before is now proved. It was assumed that Ladies would be the reason of the degradation in moral and character attributes of men. According to the assumptions done in *Brhampuran* regarding *Kaliyug*:-

स्वपोषणपराः कुद्धा देहसंस्कारवर्जिताः । पुरुषानृतभाषिण्यो
भविष्यन्ति कलौ स्त्रियः ।
दुःशीला दुष्टशीलेषु कुर्वत्यः सततं स्पृहाम् । असदृता
भविष्यन्ति पुरुषेषु कुलांगनाः ॥

In *Kaliyug*, ladies shall be involved in immoral activities and would be busy in bringing up themselves and would also be very selfish. Ladies would be careless for sanctifying rites, never speak truth and would converse brusquely. Ladies would be of vindictive disposition, eager to attain sensual pleasure and would express pseudo conduct to men in order to allure and deceive them. According to the assumption of *Kaliyug* in *Shivpuran*:-

स्त्रियश्चप्रायशोभ्रष्टाभर्त्रवज्ञानकारिकाः ।।
श्वशुरद्रोहकारिण्योनिर्भयामलिनाशनाः ।

कुत्स्वभावनिरताः कुशीलास्स्मरविह्वलाः ।।

जारसंगरतानित्यंस्वस्वामिविमुखास्तथा ।
अविद्या पाठकानित्यंरोगग्रसितदेहकाः ।।

तनयामातृपित्रोश्चभक्तिहीनादुराशयाः ।।

In *Kaliyug*, ladies shall disobey even the proper and genuine guidelines provided by their husbands. They'll keep active rivalry for the parents of their husbands. They will have daring nature for committing transgressions, would be of wicked nature and licentious tendencies, entirely devoted to attain corporeal contentment, would carry illicit physical relations with rich men thus betraying their husbands and blemish the honor of the families. The assumption regarding the ladies in *Brhampuran* is done in following way:-

सर्वेभ्य एवं वर्णेभ्यो नरः कन्योपजीविनः ।।

स्त्रीणां रूपमदश्चैव केशैरेव भविष्यति ।।

सुवर्णमणिरत्नादौ वस्त्रे चापक्षयं गते ।
कलौ स्त्रिया भविष्यन्ति तदा केशैरलंकृताः ।।
स्त्रियः कलौ भविष्यन्ति स्वैरिण्यो ललितस्पृहाः ।

श्वश्रूश्वशुरभूयिष्ठा गुरवश्च नृणां कलौ ।

शालाद्याहारिभार्याश्च सुहृदो मुनिसत्तमाः ।।
कस्य माता पिता कस्य यदा कर्मात्मकः पुमान्
इति चोदाहरिष्यन्ति श्वशुरानुगता नराः ।।
ऊनषोडशवर्षाश्च प्रसोष्यन्ति तथा स्त्रियः ।

प्रमदाः केशशूलाश्च भविष्यन्ति युगक्षये ।।

पुरुषाल्पं बहुस्त्रीकं तद्युगान्तस्य लक्षणम् ।।

प्रेषयन्ति पितृन्पुत्रा वधूः श्वश्रूः स्वकर्मसु ।।

वन्चयित्वा पतीन्सुतानामिष्यन्ति स्त्रियोऽन्यतः ।।

In *Kaliyug* people of all community will extract their living from the ladies. Parents will make their unmarried daughters to earn for them and in case of married daughters, they shall take financial support from son in laws. Ladies shall be proud of their hair and other symbols of external beauty. They shall give away the internal beauty thereby leaving morals and ethics behind. They shall leave their poor husbands and commit adultery by keeping immoral sexual relations with rich men. They shall be involved in illicit physical relations without any hesitation. Men will consider their mother in law and father-in law as their actual parents or gurus and they shall keep the sexual relations with the daughters of their gurus. Similarly teachers as guru shall keep illicit sexual relations with their female students. Men shall dishonor and neglect their own parents in front of their in-laws or wife's parents. Taking care of parents of wife, they shall disregard their own parents and say "who is whose father and who is whose mother?". Girls shall give birth to children before attaining the age of sixteen and shall involve in the debauchery either clandestinely or publicly. Ladies shall rule the residence by suppressing the qualities and rights of their virtuous husbands thereby making them mentally impotent. Sons will order their own parents and their wives to mother-in-laws to work as a slave. Wives would secretly commit harlotry while husbands would be sleeping.

# Religion On Human Characteristics

Qualities are of three kind *Satgun*, *Rajogun* and *Tamogun*. The character of men and women depends upon the above three types of qualities. According to *Mahabharath*:-

तमो रजस्तथा सत्त्वं गुणनेतान् प्रचक्षते ।
अन्योन्यमिथुनाः सर्वे तथान्योन्यानुजीविनः ॥
अन्योन्यापाश्रयाश्चपि तथान्योन्यानुवर्तिनः ।
अन्योन्यव्यतिषत्त श्च त्रिगुणाः पश्चघातवः ॥
तमसो मिथुनं सत्त्वं सत्त्वस्य मिथुनं रजः ।
रजसश्चापि सत्त्वं स्यात् सत्त्वस्य मिथुनं तमः ॥
नियम्यते तमो यत्र रजस्तत्र प्रवर्तते ।
नियम्यते रजो यत्र सत्त्वं तत्र प्रवर्तते ।
सम्मोहोऽज्ञानमत्यागः कर्मणामविनिर्णयः ।
स्वप्नः स्तम्भो भयं लोभः स्वतः सुकृतदूषणम् ॥
अस्मृतिश्चाविपाकश्च नास्तिक्यं भिन्नवृत्तिता ।
निर्विशेषत्वमन्धत्वं जघन्यगुणवृत्तिता ॥
अकृते कृतमानित्वमज्ञाने ज्ञानमानिता ।
अमैत्री विकृताभावो ह्यश्रद्धा मूढभावना ॥
अनार्जवमसंज्ञत्वं कर्म पापमचेतना ।
गुरुत्वं सत्रभावत्वमवशित्वमवाग्गतिः ॥
सर्वे एते गुणा वृत्तास्तामसाः सम्प्रकीर्तिताः ।
ये चान्ये विहिता भावा लोकेऽस्मिन्नुभावसंज्ञिताः ॥
तत्र तत्र नियम्यन्ते सर्वे ते तामसा गुणाः ।

*Satgun*, *Rajogun* and *Tamogun* are the three types of qualities. Though by nature they are the contestant to each other yet they are the adherent too. All five *Mahabhuta* are

14

followed by the joint venture of these three. The competitor of *Tamogun* is *Satgun* and competitor of *Satgun* is *Rajogun*. In the similar way competitor of *Rajogun* is *Satgun*. Thus these three sets of qualities are opposite as well as equivalent to each other. These are said to be opponent to each other because one is suppressed by the presence of other. When *Tamogun* is suppressed then effect of *Rajogun* is increased and where *Rajogun* is suppressed then *Satgun* comes in effect.

Over attachment towards sensual pleasure, ignorance, egotism, imprudence, excessive sleeping, arrogance, trepidation, avarice, finding oversight in virtuous act performed by others, lack of memory, lack of discriminate between appropriate and inappropriate, not believing in God, loose character, lack of taking right decision, looseness of senses, sadistic nature, mind diverted to obtain physical happiness performing sinful deeds by considering them as good deeds, animosity, performing righteous act without willing, infidelity, stupidity, wickedness, dullness, involved in transgression, indolence, lack of devotion, lack of control over senses and involvement in awful deeds are works of *Tamogun* and are not virtuous. On the subject of *Rajogun* it is said in *Mahabharath*:-

प्रकृत्यात्मकमेवाहू रजः पर्यायकारकम् ।
प्रवृत्तं सर्वभूतेषु दृश्यमुत्पत्तिलक्षणम् ।।
सन्तापो रूपमायासः सुखदुःखे हिमातपौ ।

ऐश्वर्ये विग्रहः संधिर्हेतुवादोऽरतिः क्षमा ।।
बलं शौर्ये मदो रोषो व्यायामकलहावपि ।
ईर्ष्येप्सा पिशुनं युद्धं ममत्वं परिपालनम् ।।
वघबन्धपरिक्लेशाः क्रयो विक्रय एव च ।
निकृन्त छिन्धि भिन्धीति परमर्मावकर्तनम् ।
उग्रं दारुणमाक्रोशः परच्छिद्रानुशासनम् ।
लोकचिन्तानुविन्ता च मत्सरः परिभावनः ।
मृषा वादो मृषा दानं विकल्पः परिभाषणम् ।
निन्दा स्तुतिः प्रशंसा च प्रस्तावः पारधर्षणम् ।।

Again it is said in *Bhagwat Gita*:-

काम एष क्रोध एष रजोगुणसमुद्भवः ।
महाशनो महापाप्मा विद्ध्येनमिह वैरिणम् ।।

The whole world is surviving on the basis of quality i.e. *Rajogun*, an actual appearance of nature. The visible site of the world is the form of *Rajogun*. Sorrow, beauty, command, grief- pleasure, summer-winter, prosperity, severance, negotiation, sophistry, happiness, power of endurance, supremacy, audacity, proud, annoyance, physical exercise, conflict, jealousy, desire, treachery, zeal for combat, parental affection, governing family duties, assassination, limitations or restrictions or obligations or ritual confinements, intense abhorrence, purchasing or selling, piercing, conspiracy, attempt for tearing or autopsy of living or dead, hurting the feelings of someone, aggressiveness, harshness of manner or emotionless, harsh speaking, criticizing others, seeking sensual pleasure only, speaking lie, showing fake charity,

16

skepticism, scolding others, admiring someone, magnificence, sexual molestation, to attend a sick person with egotism, serving elders with noble cause, torment of desire, parasite nature, nimbleness, diplomacy, profligacy, censure and self-indulgence  are the symptoms of *Rajogun*. It is said by Lord Krishna in *Gita* that human being commits sin because of the greed for sensual pleasure which in turn is due to *Rajogun*. This kind of sensual pleasure ultimately produces antagonism in human which is the most powerful enemy of human being as it vanishes the discretion power and conscience. According to *Mahabharat*, *Satgun* is defined as:-

प्रकाशं सर्वभूतेषु लाघवं श्रद्धधानता ।
सात्त्विकं रूपमेव तु लाघवं साधुसम्मितम् ॥
आनन्दः प्रीतिरुद्रेकः प्राकाश्यं सुखमेव च ।
अकार्पण्यमसंरम्भः सन्तोषः श्रद्धधानता ॥
क्षमा धृतिरहिंसा च समता सत्यमार्जवम् ।
अक्रोधश्चनसूया च शौचं दाक्ष्यं पराक्रमः ॥
विश्रम्भो ह्रीस्तितिक्षा च त्याग शौचमतन्द्रिता ।
आनृशंस्यमसम्मोहो दया भूतेष्वपैशुनम् ॥
हर्षस्तुष्टिर्विस्मयश्च विनयः साधुवृत्तिता ।
शान्तिकर्मणि शुद्धिश्च शुभा बुद्धिर्विमोचनम् ॥
उपेक्षा ब्रह्मचर्यं च परित्यागश्च सर्वशः ।
निर्ममत्वमनाशीष्टमपरिक्षतधर्मता ॥

The form of *Satgun* delights the senses and comes out from the inner of hearty feelings in the form of reverence for others. Pleasure, happiness, enthusiasm, comfort, feeling of pettiness, braveness, satisfaction, respect, mercy, endurance,

17

nonviolence, egalitarianism, honesty, minimalism, seeking and then eradicating own faults instead of blaming others, cleanliness, purity, practical wisdom and courageousness are the properties of *Satgun*.

Faith, introversion, endurance, sacrifice, wholesomeness, perception, gentleness, minor temptation for corporeal matters, forgiveness, not passing the personal talks of a particular person to others, internal happiness, satisfaction, lack of arrogance, graciousness, performing duties for a living as well as for a deceased relative with purity and devotion, maintaining virginity, sacrificing own happiness for the sake of others, cruelly suppressing own desire for immoral sensual pleasure, believing on self caliber not on destiny and worshipping God are the qualities of *Satgun*. According to *Gita* Lord Sri *Krishna* says:-

सत्त्वं सुखे सन्जयति रज: कर्मणि भारत।
ज्ञानमावृत्स तु तम: प्रमादे सन्जयत्युत।।
ऊर्ध्वं गच्छन्ति सत्त्वस्था मध्ये तिष्ठन्ति राजसा:।
जघन्यगुणवृत्तिस्था अधो गच्छन्ति तामसा:।।
सत्त्वात्सन्जयते ज्ञानं रजसो लोभ एव च।
प्रमादमोहौ तमसो भवतोऽज्ञानमेव च।।
रजसि प्रलयं गत्वा कर्मसगिषु जायते।
तथा प्रलीनस्तमसि मूढयोनिषु जायते।।
यदा सत्त्वे प्रवृद्धे तु प्रलयं याति देहभृत्।
तदोत्तमविदां लोकानमलान्प्रतिपद्यते।।
यजन्ते सात्त्विका देवान्यक्षरक्षांसि राजसा:।
प्रेतान्भूतगणांश्चान्ये यजन्ते तामसा जना:।।

*Satgun* attaches a person with real happiness, *Rajogun* attaches him with his sensual duties and *Tamogun* attaches a person with lack of knowledge thus invoking in him a kind of mental perversion. A person having S*atgun* occupies heaven after death, people having *Rajogun* occupy earth in different incarnations after the death and people carrying *Tamogun* are sent to the hell. *Satgun* produces actual knowledge, *Rajogun* produces greediness while *Tamogun* produces lack of knowledge, intoxication and immoral sensual affection. In case of *Rajogun*, after death on reincarnation, a person gets human birth on earth but in case of *Tamogun*, after death a person obtains either the form of other creatures or the hell and in case of *Satgun* after death person becomes free from the cycle of life and death thus attains the planet of God. Prayer service of a *Satguni* or a follower of *Satgun* is delivered to God whereas prayer of a *Rajoguni* or the follower of *Rajogun* is offered to monsters while prayer of a *Tamoguni* is devoted to evil spirits. According to *Devi Bhagwat Mahapuran*:-

सत्त्वं सुखे सन्जयति रज: कर्मणि भारत।
ज्ञानमावृत्य तु तम: प्रमादे सन्जयत्युत।।
ऊर्ध्वं गच्छन्ति सत्त्वस्था मध्ये तिष्ठन्ति राजसा:।
जघन्यगुणवृत्तिस्था अधो गच्छन्ति तामसा:।।

सत्त्वात्सञ्जयते ज्ञानं रजसो लोभ एव च।
प्रमादमोहौ तमसो भवतोऽज्ञानमेव च।।
रजसि प्रलयं गत्वा कर्मसङ्गिषु जायते।
तथा प्रलीनस्तमसि मूढयोनिषु जायते।।
यदा सत्त्वे प्रवृद्धे तु प्रलयं याति देहभृत्।
तदोत्तमविदां लोकानमलान्प्रतिपद्यते।।
यजन्ते सात्त्विका देवान्यक्षरक्षांसि राजसाः।
प्रेतान्भूतगणांश्चान्ये यजन्ते तामसा जनाः।।

Satgun indicates the true affection and is the prime reason for the upcoming of factual love. Thus the unblemished contentment or immortal pleasure is also the form of Satgun. Truth, purity, politeness, paying reverence, forgiveness, serenity, coyness and gratification are the forms of Satgun. The color of Satgun is white and it indicates love for God. It shows the raising of factual love and diminishing of sensual love. Hence the true love can also be termed as devotion to noble cause. Devotion could be divided into three parts:- Satwik, Rajsi and Tamsi. Satwik devotion is of white color, immortal and feeling less. Rajsi devotion indicates the red color and denotes the symbol of extraordinary sensual love. This typical love which is the reason of sorrow is the part of the Rajsi devotion. To obtain the love forcefully at any cost becomes the reason of sorrow. Where Rajsi devotion is diverted towards immoral track, becomes the cause of Jealousy, abhor, hostility, eagerness and luxury. The reason of pseudo ego, arrogance and mental perversion is Rajsi devotion. The color of *Tamsi* devotion is black. It is the symbol of illicit sensual relations and painful sorrow. Laziness, excessive sleep, poverty, fear, anguish, cowardice, shrewdness, annoyance, distortion, blasphemy and captious criticism are the symptoms of *Tamsi* devotion. *Tamsi* devotion creates a perversion in human mind and effected person feels happy to trouble others.

# Nomenclature of Women

There is a wide description regarding nomenclature of ladies on the basis of there virtuous and awful qualities. Ten types of women are mentioned in *Bhavishya Puran*:-

समुद्रभूषितचारित्रा गुरूभह्या पतिव्रता।
देवब्राह्यणभक्ता च मानुषीं तां विनिर्दिशेत्।।
नित्यं स्नाता सुगन्धा च नित्यं च प्रियवादिनी।
अल्पाशिन्यल्परोषा च देवतां तां विनिर्दिशेत्।।
प्रच्छन्नं कुरूते पापमपवादं च रक्षति।
हृदयं स्याच्च दुर्ग्राह्यं मार्जारीं तां विनिर्दिशेत्।।
हसते क्रीडते चैव कुध्दा चैव प्रसीदति।
नीचेषु रमते नित्यं रासभीं तां विनिर्दिशेत्।।
प्रतिकूलकरी नित्यं बन्धूनां क्षतुरेव च।
स्वच्छन्दे ललितां चैव आसुरीं तां विनिर्दिशेत्।।
बह्व्यांशी बहुवाक्या च नित्यं चाप्रियवादिनी।
हिनस्ति स्वपतिं या तु राक्षसीं तां विनिर्दिशेत्।।
शौचाचारपरिभ्रष्टा रूपभ्रष्टा भयङ्करा।
प्रस्वेदमलपङ्का च पिशाचीं तां विनिर्दिशेत्।।
नित्यं स्नातां सुगन्धां च मांसमद्यप्रियादिनीम्।
वृक्षोद्यानप्रसक्ता च गान्धर्वीं तां विनिर्दिशेत्।।
चपला चन्चला चैव नित्यं पश्येक्तिशस्तथा।
चलस्वभावा लुब्धा च वानरीं तां विनिर्दिशेत्।।
चन्द्राननां शुभांगी तु मत्तवारणगामिनीम्।
आरक्तनखहस्तां तु विद्याद्विद्याधरीं बुधः।।

Ladies who are of very noble character, pay respect to elders and teachers and obey their husbands of virtuous conduct are called as *Manusi*.

Ladies who regularly take bath thereby keeping physical cleanliness, use perfume, converse very courteously, consume just sufficient food and do not loose the temperament are said to be *Devta*.

Ladies who commit transgression like keeping illicit physical relations clandestinely and perform immoral acts while protect themselves from probable defame caused by those acts and whose internal feeling could not be understand very easily are said to be *Marjari* or black cat.

Ladies who express the undue resentment as well as contentment in performing any kind of sensual activity and are found to be attracted towards those men and women, who are involved in appalling deeds, are said to be *Rashbhi* or donkey.

Ladies who always work against the right guidelines given to them by their husbands, brothers or parents and carry immoral sexual relations freely like a prostitute are said to be *Asuri* or demoness.

Ladies who eat a lot, are very talkative, speak harshly and torture their husbands physically or mentally are called *Rakshasi* or devil.

Ladies who are diverted from norms of purity and morality, wicked by nature and do not hate disgusting things and relations are called *Pishachi* or evil.

Ladies who take bath regularly, put face pack or perfumed body lotions, consume meat and alcoholic beverages as per their liking and frequently enjoy by roaming about in gardens and parks are called *Gandharvi*.

Ladies having capricious nature, fickle eyes, watching here and there to men by twisted eye balls, inconsistent tendency and extreme greedy nature are called *Vanari* or female monkey.

Ladies having shining faces like moon, body decorated by ominous symptoms, particular gait like an elephant, beautiful reddish nails and palms are said to be *Vidyadhari*.

Again in *Bhavishya Puran* the classification of women is done on behalf of their feminine nature and age:-

असम्प्राप्तरजा गौरी प्राप्ते रजसि रोहिणी।
अव्यंजनयुता कन्या कुचहीना च नग्रिका।।
सप्तवर्षा भवेद्गौरी दशवर्षा तु नग्रिका।
द्वादशे तु भवेत्कन्या अत ऊर्ध्वं रजस्वला।।

A girl who is not *Ritumati* or whose menses have not started yet, is said to be *Gauri*.

*Rajaswala* or whose menses have started is termed as *Rohini*.

*Vyanjanheena* or a girl without maturity symptoms is called *Kanya*.

A girl whose breast and other symptoms have not developed yet is said to be *Nagnika*.

Thus a girl of seven years old is called *Gauri*, while a girl of ten years is called *Nagnika*, a girl of twelve years old is called *kanya*, and above this age is called *Ritumati*. Nomenclature of girls on the basis of age in *Devi Bhagwat Mahapuran* is as follows:-

कुमारिका तु सा प्रोक्ता द्विवर्षा या भवेदिह ।
त्रिमूर्तिश्च त्रिवर्षा च कल्याणी चतुरब्दिका ।।
रोहिणी पन्चवर्षा च षड्वर्षा कालिका स्मृता ।
चण्डिका सप्तवर्षा स्यादष्टवर्षा च शाम्भवी ।।
नववर्षा भवेद्दुर्गा सुभद्रा दशवार्षिकी ।
श्रत ऊर्ध्व न कर्तव्या सर्वकार्यविगहिता ।।

Girl who has completed the two years of age is said to be *kumari kanya*. A Girl of three years age is said to be *Trimurti*. A girl of four years is called *Kalyani*, five years is called *Rohini*, six years is called *Kalika*, seven years is called *chandika*, eight years old girl is said to be *Shambhawi*, nine years old is *Durga* and ten years old is called *Subhadra*. Above the age of ten years, girls are said to be *Rajaswala*. In the state of being *Rajaswala* they are no more worshiped in religious service. The girls worshiped in sacred ceremonies lie from two years to ten years age.

Husband devoting women are classified by four parts in *Shiv Puran*. Women are said to be husband devotee, if they do not commit sexual relations said to be as *Gaman* with any man other than their respective husband. Just by remembering such women one can get rid from the transgressions that he committed in his life span as such women are equivalent to goddess because of their sanctified character. For a woman any man other than her husband is termed as *Agamya*. Similarly for a man any woman other than his wife is termed as *Agamya*. Sexual relations with *Agamya* are illicit and immoral. Aforesaid four classifications of virtuous women are done in *Shiv Puran* on the basis of the situations under which they keep their chastity maintained:-

चतुर्विधास्ताः कथिता नार्यो देवि पतिव्रताः ॥
उत्तमादिविभेदेन स्मरतां पापहारिकाः ॥
उत्तमा मध्या चैव निकृष्टातिनिकृष्टिका ॥
ब्रुवे तासां लक्षणानि सावधानतया शृणु ॥
स्वप्नेपि यन्मनो नित्यं स्वपतिं पश्यति ध्रुवम् ॥
नान्यम्परपतिं भद्रे उत्तमा सा प्रकीर्तिता ॥
यापितृभ्रातृसुतवत् परम्पश्यति सद्धिया ॥
मध्यमा सा हि कथिता शैलजेवै पतिव्रता ॥
बुद्ध्या स्वधर्मे मनसा व्यभिचारं करोति न ॥
निकृष्टा कथिता सा हि सुचरित्रा च पार्वति ॥
पत्युः कुलस्य च भयाद्व्यभिचारं करोति न ॥
पतिव्रताऽधमा सा हि कथिता पूर्वसूरिभिः ॥

A lady who never even thinks about a man other than her husband even in her dreams is said to be *Uttam Pativrata* or best husband devotee.

A lady who finds other men of the world considering them as her father, brother or son is said to be *Madhyam Pativrata* or medium level husband devotee.

A lady who keeps herself away from illicit sexual relations due to religious fear is said to be *Nikrisht Pativrata* or worse husband devotee.

A lady who does not carry illicit physical relations even after having keen sexual desire for lust because of fear of husband and his dynasty is said to be *Ati Nikrisht Pativrata* or worst husband devotee.

In *Bhavishya Puran* women are classified on the basis of their character in the following way:-

कन्या पुनर्भूर्वेश्या च त्रिविधा एव योषितः ।
प्रिया मध्याप्रिया चैव योग्या मध्येतरा तथा ।।

On the basis of a woman's psychology regarding virtuousness of character and sexual relations, she is considered as *Kanya* or *Punarbhu* or V*ashya*. As per the nature of lady and her view about men, it is said that for a husband *Kanya* means loving, *Punarbhu* means medium loving and *Vashya* means least loving wife. Here *Kanya* is said for a lady who does not keep any sexual feelings or relations with any other man except her husband whereas by

27

*Punarbhu*, it means a lady who has kept or carries the physical relations before or after her marriage with any man other than her husband. A lady who keeps sexual relation with any person for money is called *Vashya*.

In *Devi Bhagwat Mahapuran* the nomenclature of ladies is done on the basis of number of husbands. Here number of husbands means the count of men with which a woman carries the feeling of husband regarding sexual relations at a time.

पतिव्रता चैकपतौ द्वितीये कुलटा स्मृता ।
तृतीये धर्षिणी ज्ञेया चतुर्थे पुंश्चलीत्यपि ।।
वेश्या च पन्चमे, षष्ठे पुटगी च सप्तमेऽष्टमे ।
तत ऊर्ध्वं महावेश्या सास्पृश्या सर्वजातिषु ।।
यो द्विज: कुलटां गच्छेद्धर्षिणीं पुंश्चलीमपि ।
पुंगी वेश्यां महावेश्यां मत्स्योदे याति निश्चितम् ।।

Lady with one husband is said to be *Pativrata* or woman with virtuous character. A lady with two husbands is said *Kulta*. Wife with three husbands is called *Gharshini*. Wife of four husbands is called *Punshchali*. Wife of five or six husbands is called *Vashya*. Wife of seven or eight husbands is called *Pungi*. Wife of more than eight husbands is called *Maha Vashya*. Out of these, a man who sexually intercourses with a lady belonging to any of the last six categories, go to hell after death termed as *Matsyadan* hell. On the basis of the requirement of the result of the religious prayer service stated in *Devi Bhagwat Mahapuran*, the age of girls who are worshiped and their nomenclature according to their age is mentioned. In the religious prayer of goddess *Bhagwati*, these girls are worshipped at the occasion of *Navratri*.

कुमारी पूजिता कुर्याद्दुःखदारिद्र यनाशनम् ।
शत्रुक्षयं धनायुष्यं बलवृद्धिं करोति वे ।।
त्रिमूर्तिपूजनादायुस्त्रिवर्गस्य फलं भवेत् ।
धनधान्यागमश्चैव पुत्रपौत्रादिवृद्धयः ।।
विद्यार्थी विजयार्थी च राज्यार्थं यश्च पार्थिवः ।
सुखार्थी पूज्येत्रितयं कल्याणी सर्वकामदाम् ।।
कालिकां शत्रुनाशार्थ पूज्येकिपूर्वकम् ।
ऐश्वर्यधनकामश्च चरांडकां परिपूजयेत् ।।
पूजयेच्छाम्भवीं नित्यं नृपसम्मोहनाय च ।
दुःखदारिद्रयनाशाय संग्रामे विजयाय च ।।
क्रूरशत्रुविनाशार्थ तथोग्रकर्म-साधने ।।
दुर्गा च पूजयेदभतथा परलोकसुखाय च ।।
वाञ्छितार्थस्य सिद्ध्यर्थ सुभद्रां पूजयेत्तदा
रोहिणी रोगनाशाय पूजयेद्विचिवत्ररः ।।

Objective to worship *Kumari* is to diminish poverty, destroy enemy and increase of the age and power. Worshipping *Trimurti* increases money, agricultural wealth and number of offspring. Worshipping *Kalyani* is done for attaining victory, higher education and paramount power. *Kalika* is worshipped for subduing enemies. *Chandika* is worshipped for the increment of wealth and prosperity. *Shambhwai* is worshipped to impress the king and achieving victory in the battle. *Durga* is worshipped to destroy cruel powerful enemies. *Subhadra* is worshipped for accomplishing any heart's desire

29

and *Rohine* is worshipped to get cured from any kind of sickness or diseases. The above classification of girls has already been done earlier on the basis of their ages. Again *Kanya* is considered for a girl of two years and rest of girl's types has the age added by one year respectively.

## Analysis of women on the basis of physical symptoms

There is a wide description of the symptoms like nature, tendency and destiny of women on the basis of their physical attributes done in *Bhavishya Puran*:-

प्रतिष्ठिततलौ सम्यग्रताम्भोजसमप्रभौ ।
ईदृशौ चरणौ धन्यौ योषितां भोगवर्धनौ ।।
करालैरतिनिर्मांसै रूक्षैरर्धशिरान्वितै:
दारिद्रयं दुर्भगत्वं च प्राप्नुवन्ति न संशय: ।।
अङ्गुल्य: संहता वृत्ता: स्निधा: सूक्ष्मनखास्तथा ।
कुर्वन्त्यत्यन्तमैश्चर्यं राजभावं च योषित: ।।

— — — — — — — — — — —


मृदूनि मृदुरोमाणि नात्यन्तस्वेदकानि च ।
सुरभीणि च गात्राणि यासां ता: पूजिता: स्त्रिय: ।।

Ladies having beautiful attractive soles of red color resembling just like leaf of lotus flower have a bright future as such soles are the indication of peak positive rise in their destiny. Ladies whose soles are fleshless and dry skinned with visible veins are the symbol of poverty and bad fortune.

Ladies whose fingers of legs are close to each other, rounded and smooth with beautiful nails are the symbol of wealth and bring prosperity to family. Small fingers of legs bring longevity of life to ladies whereas short fingers which are not close to each other indicates financial crisis in family as

31

such type of ladies on birth at father's place and after marriage at husband place bring financial loss. Tilted fingers at the base are the symbol of poverty whereas fatty fingers indicate slavery. Ladies having very tiny and thin fingers overlapping each other and rounded at the end points become the reason of death of number of husbands. Ladies with high peaked ends of soft fingers are very fortunate and have the capability to find gold or precious things even in the soil or useless things, while ladies having opposite natured fingers of feet become the cause of lots of problems in the family.

Ladies with soft and smooth nails bring fortune while ladies with red colored nails bring wealth to families. Ladies with long peaked nails give birth to number of sons while one with short nails provides royal status to their husbands. Ladies having broken, yellow colored, dry, blue colored, faint or abnormal shaped nails bring poverty in the family. Ladies specially having yellow nails eat even inedible items.

In context of rise of ankle, it would be said that a lady with smooth and round ankle where nerves are not visible due to flesh, always brings prosperity and melodious environment in her family like the ringing sound of an anklets and is accompanied by many brothers.

In context of thighs it is said that the ladies with invisible nerves due to flesh, fair, attractive, beautifully curved and with less hair on thighs bring good fortune to their families as they are the symbol of royalty. Ladies having thick, long or plenty of hair on the thighs bring problems for themselves and for their family members. Ladies whose calf of the leg or muscles of thighs carry strain towards upward are found to be roaming here and there, thereby making their life unsteady. Ladies of whitish color complexion having thighs like the shape of a crow are very garrulous, speak bitterly, and are very dangerous for the life of husbands.

In context of knees it is said that ladies having knees like cat or lion bring prosperity and wealth to family because of being the form of goddess *Laxmi* and give birth to number of sons. Ladies with knees like a pitcher, love to go for excursion and like to stay out of house. Ladies with fleshless thighs are found to be involved in illicit sexual relations. Ladies with visible blood vessels on knees are of very violent nature while those having thin and ugly knees are the symbol of poverty. The ladies who have very dry skinned knees, distorted from front, reddish in color with many hair growing from single pour and ladies of yellow colored complexion act as poison to their husband and become the reason for death of husband within a week after marriage.

In context with the lower belly part or abdominal area, it is said that ladies with belly having smooth peak and downs like the trunk of an elephant or whitish color like a plantain fruit or unwrapped banana and downy with attractive in looking are blessed by the lord of adore and sex, *Kamdeva*. Ladies having the belly portion looking just like embedded with flesh pieces bring extreme bad fortune to family. Ladies with lot of visible long or thick hair on this portion of the body lead a life of dependency or slavery. Ladies having tiny or small belly portion die unexpectedly. Ladies who have the tiny holes on the middle of the outer abdominal part loose the control over others hence possess no attraction to influence others. Ladies having wide belly portion, pleasant like the calmness of a beautiful evening with very small hardly visible hair on it, become the center of attraction among men and provide great sexual pleasure to them.

In context to *Yoni* or vaginal portion, it is stated that if the *Yoni* portion is hairless with symmetrical, proper and attractive joints then such lady even if born in poverty occupies the prosperity and fame. Ladies having *Yoni* just like the leaf of *Pipal tree* and peaked rising up like the back of tortoise equivalent in appearance to mirage of moon looking like a pitcher are very fortunate and provide extreme sexual pleasure. Ladies with *Yoni* looking like flower of sesame plant or raised like hoof of an animal have the life of poverty and slavery. *Yoni* just like floating aromatic resin provides distress to ladies. Ladies having wide opening of vaginal path of *Yoni* are the symbol of death for their respective husbands. Ladies with *Yoni* looking ugly, unappealing, stinking, and fleshless with long hair like a lady elephant bring poverty and bad fortune to their family. Ladies with healthy and fleshly *Yoni* like the fruit wood apple and very smooth without any shrink or wrinkle are admired by men.

In context of the middle part or upper stomach or portion above navel, it is said that three wrinkles formed on the middle part of body because of heavy peaked breasts with very less and tiny hair, bring prosperity and happiness. Ladies having the middle part of the body just like a small drum or crumbly soil or grain of barley have a nature to be frightened unnecessarily and due to not having a permanent residence are always found to be in trouble.

In context of buttocks it is said that bent less, symmetrically curved without any sharp tilt, straight so that not rising upwards and hairless buttocks of ladies are admired and such women attract people while standing, sitting and moving.

A lady who has hump on the back or a hunchbacked women with unattractive and hairy back do not attain happiness and satisfaction even in the dreams and always quarrel and beat her husband and be the main cause of making conflicts among others.

Ladies having visible womb portion or stomach or portion below navel being soft and wide, give birth to number of infants. Women having stomach like the stomach of frog give birth to sons with destiny to be a king. If the lines of shrink or wrinkles on the stomach are peaked and clearly visible then such women are barren hence unable to conceive. Incase these lines are rounded making deep curve then such ladies are involved in illicit sexual relations and always carry extra marital affairs.

Ladies, whose peaked breasts are little bent downward, are of courteous nature and admired by men while those who have one breast tending towards up and other towards down are of nasty mindset and unsympathetic behavior. Those having the normal and equally leveled breasts attain prosperity and long life.

Ladies having the well shaped beautifully curved fleshy breasts with smooth peak appearing to be dense and rectangular, lead a happy life and admired by others while ladies with opposite of above qualities of breasts lead a sorrowful life. During the first pregnancy if there is growth in any of the breast, they have different meanings. If right breast grows more then a girl takes birth and if left breast grows more then a boy takes birth. Ladies having long nipples are said to be very cunning and always involved in illicit sexual relations. If the nipples are round and big enough then the wife proves herself to be keeping malicious intentions for husband. If the nipples are like the expanded hood of snake or tongue of dog then those ladies are of masculine nature and are the symbol of poverty. Ladies having breasts like small pitcher have to do physical labor like men for earning and live in destitution. The ladies with right and left fleshy breast being mirror image of each other with no visible veins or hair on it provide great pleasure during sexual intercourse. Ladies having distorted breast are of violent nature. Ladies having hairy breasts are found to be characterless and unfortunate hence are the symbol of distress and grief. Women with almost fleshless breast carry widowhood in early period of their marital life. Women with wide breasts are found to be very cunning and quarrelsome natured.

In context of the fingers of hands it is said that women having beautiful fingers, uniformly curved at the end pores, thin towards the pores, covered with soft skin and symmetrical in appearance are destined to provide wealth and extreme sensual pleasure. Ladies having very reddish nails which are bit risen upwards, experience prosperity in their life. Ladies with distorted or colorless or whitish or yellowish nails bring disaster and blemish the royal status of their families. Women having reddish, soft and pour less fingers on the soft palm bring prosperity while women with distorted and dissimilar fingers with rough skinned palm become the reason of tribulation and conflicts. Those women who have healthy, fleshy and hairless arms without visible blood vessels are found to be fortunate. Ladies having the tissues of elbow joint covered with flesh, hairless hands and soft arms are admired by people. Ladies having the properly shaped arms without excessive flesh and hairless hands bring opulence and good health in husband's life. If both the shoulders of a lady are heavy shaped and tough then she has to do physical work like carrying load of luggage like a labor. Ladies having hairy shoulders suffer from diseases during whole of their life. Distorted or unshaped shoulders denote barrenness in ladies while those who have difference in the level of shoulders are found to be involved in illicit sexual relations.

If a lady has three lines in between the width of her four fingers on her neck then she is very prosperous and possesses ample of gold or precious jewelries. If the neck of the lady is very thin then she lives in poverty. A woman with very long neck is always involved in prostitution. Kids of a woman with very short neck die unexpectedly. A woman with very fleshy and heavy neck experiences problems in life. If in the middle of neck, rising part of throat bone is symmetrical and flashy then such woman lives a long life and this even helps on increasing longevity of the life of her husband too. Extreme flashy throat with rising of nerves does not indicate happiness in the life of a woman.

In context of chin it is said that a chin being heavy like double chin, very thin, tilted looking unsymmetrical and being hairy are not the symbols of virtuous personality. Ladies who possess square shaped face are very astute natured. Ladies having round shaped face spread factual love and blessings among others. Ladies having face like horse mouth are barren while those having extraordinary long face are unfortunate. Women resembling their face with dog, pig, wolf, owl and monkey are of very cruel nature, diverted towards committing unforgivable sins, barren and do not have any brothers. Ladies whose mouth fragrances like flowers of jasmine, *Maulagiri*, lotus, and blue lotus always get the high quality food and live a rich and prosperous life. Ladies with reddish, soft, medium flashy or without excessive thickness or thinness and little risen upward lips always experience sensual pleasure. Ladies with thick lips are fond of arguing unnecessarily and are of quarrelsome nature. Ladies who have colorless or faint lips experience sorrow in the whole span of their life. If the upper lip is thin in comparison to lower lip then such ladies are very aggressive.

A tongue with thin, symmetrical curved, long and reddish appearance gives the sign of contentment while thick, short, randomly tilted and colorless tongues are not considered to be auspicious in ladies. A harrow, appearing like conch shell, golden flower, having glory of moon, smooth and gapless with adjoining teeth, provides luxury and pleasure to ladies. Ladies with very short, weak, fractured, dry, distorted and abnormal looking teeth experience trouble and are inauspicious. Ladies with clean and attractive face looking like mirror or lotus or mirage of full moon always achieve their desire and are always favored by their destiny. If the nose of a lady is medium flashy thereby in-between heavy and thin size with medium length then she spreads blessing among people and be auspicious for herself as well as for others. Peaked, soft and properly alienated short eyebrows provide happiness and sensual pleasure to ladies. Eyebrows tilted like a bow bring prosperity. Long hairy eyebrows indicate the sterility in a lady. Yellow colored, unsymmetrical and short eyebrows are the symbol of poverty. Beautiful naturally decorated reddish eyebrows attractive like the petal of blue lotus bring sensual pleasure and prosperity in ladies. Ladies having eyes like birds, deer, or a swine may born in any wealthy or deprived family but ultimately they become wealthy and achieve prosperity. Ladies with eyes reddish like honey, showing attitude of insincerity and fickle gesture have bright future to rule on others.

Eyes like a crow, sharp cornered, clean and beautiful bring the possibilities of success and wealth in the life of women. Ladies having yellow colored and utterly sincere looking eyes live a long but sorrowful life. A woman with thick elevated eye bowls dies in the early period of the life. One should not carry any type of get-to-gather with a woman of reddish, abnormal looking or unsymmetrical, faint colored and ghost like eyes. A person should not even converse with the lady having eyes like dogs. Ladies having tilted eyes or squint eyes or whose eye balls keep moving without having natural consistency eat a lot preferring non vegetarian meal and wine and are found to be corrupt in sexual relations.

Ladies with long ears like a projection experience wealthy life. Ladies having ears like the ears of an ass, camel, mongoose or an owl with reddish-brown in color like the color of a monkey experience lot of distress and are always of roaming tendency because of their fickle nature.

Round cheeks of yellowish-white or pale color are considered to be best in women. Women with unattractive cheeks having hair and pores are impure or characterless. Forehead looking like half moon, hairless, properly shaped or symmetrical and attractive provides sensual pleasure and good health to ladies. Ladies with broad forehead like an elephant are not worthy of acclamation. Thin, black, soft, little bit curly and long hair is auspicious for ladies. Ladies having voice like a duck, black cuckoo, *vina* or lute, black bee, peacock and pipe flute enjoy extreme pleasure and affluent wealth whereas those, having voice similar to the sound produced by hitting a cracked bronze utensil or like the voice of donkey or a crow bring infirmity, anguish, fear and poverty to family.

Ladies, who walk like a swan, cow, bull, *Brahminy* bird or Ruddy Sheldrake and drunken elephant bring prosperity and achieve fame in their community while those who walk like dog, jackal and crow are scolded by others and bring defame to family. Ladies, who walk like a deer, live a life as a slave and always involved in illicit sexual relations. Ladies having body with color complex like *Mehandi* or extract of heena plant, turmeric, gold, saffron or yellow colored like pistil of crocus flower and jasmine flower bring prosperity and are auspicious to the family. Ladies with fair complexion like sprout of soft grass always experience contentment in their life. Ladies with soft, attractive and less hairy body with balanced sweat from pores are praised. Taking decision to marry with a girl on the basis of her physical qualities, it is said that person should not marry with a girl who is of very brownish or yellow complexion, suffering from incurable disease or physically very weak, with more parts of any organ in comparison to a normal body as more than five fingers etc, of hairless body or pore less body, of very short height, very talkative and of yellow-reddish or tawny complex. One should not marry with a girl whose name is kept after the name of any river, tree, star, mountain, bird, snake and a family servant or resembling with any awful name. One should marry with a lady of attractive and balanced figured body, decorated with beautiful name, who walks like duck or a female elephant, with tiny hair on the body and who has small teeth symmetrically arranged. One should not consider a girl to be appropriate for marriage even if she belongs to a very prosperous family if she or her family have either of the following ten symptoms as effortlessness or indolence, lack of self respect, distrust on religious saying or atheistic, over hairy body, suffering from piles, suffering from tuberculosis, suffering from epilepsy, very thin or always being sick due to disease, suffering from white leprosy and aggravated type leprosy. The preference to the symptoms of physical beauty depending on the body organs is given in the following way: Firstly foot and ankles of women are considered. Secondly knees and thighs are considered. Third priority is given to lower belly part or abdominal area and genital organs as vaginal area. Fourth priority is given to women with more beautiful waist and navel area. Fifth rank is given to stomach. Breast is considered at sixth place while considering the beauty of women. Shoulders are considered to be at seventh place and the next rank is given to the lips. Eyes decorated with beautiful eyebrows is provided ninth place and on judging beauty of women forehead are considered at tenth place.

According to *Bhavishya puran* a lady could be scrutinized on the account of her physical qualities before marriage in the following ways:-

हस्तौ पादौ परीक्षेत अङ्गुलीर्नखमेव च।
पाणिमेव च जङ्घे च कटिनासोरू एवं च जघनोदरपृष्ठं
च स्तनो कर्णौ भुजौ तथा।
जिह्वां चोष्ठौ च दन्ताश्च कपोलं गलकं तथा।।
चक्षुर्नासा ललाटं च शिरः कोशांस्तथैव च।
रोमराजिं स्वरं वर्णमावर्तानि तु वा पुनः।।
यस्यास्तु रेखाग्रीवायां या च रक्तान्तलोचना।
यस्य सा गृहमागच्छेक्तद्गृहं सुखमेधते।।
ललाटे दृश्यते यस्तास्त्रिशूलं देवनिर्मितम्।
बहूनां स्त्रीसहस्राणां स्वामिनीं तां विनिर्दिशेत्।।
राजहंसगतिर्यस्या मृगाक्षी मृगवर्णिका।
समशुक्लाग्रदन्ता च कन्यां तामुक्तमां विदुः।।

मण्डूककुक्षी या कन्या न्यग्रोधपरिमण्डला ।
एकं जनयते पुत्रं सोऽपि राजा भविष्यति ।।
हंसस्वरा मृदुवचा या कन्या मधुपिङ्गला ।
अष्टौ जनयते पुत्रान्धनधान्यविवर्धिनी ।।
आयतौ श्रवणौ यस्याः सुरूपा चापि नासिका ।
भ्रुवौ चेन्द्रायुधाकारौ सात्यन्तं सुखभागिनी ।।
तन्वी श्यामा तथा कृष्णा स्निग्धाङ्गी मृदुभाषिणी ।
शङ्कुन्देन्दुदशना भवेदैर्यभागिनी ।।
विस्तीर्णं जघनं यस्या वेदिमध्या तु या भवेत् ।
आयते विपुले नेत्रे राजपत्नी तु सा भवेत् ।।
यस्याः पयोधरे वामे हस्तेकर्णे गलेऽपि वा ।
मशकं तिलकं वापिसा पूर्वं जनयेत्सुतम् ।।
गूढगुल्फाङ्गुलिशिरा अल्पपार्ष्णिः सुमध्यमा ।
रक्ताक्षी रक्तचरणा सात्यन्तं सुखभागिनी ।।
कूर्मपृष्ठायतनखौ स्निग्धभावविवर्जितौ ।
वक्राङ्गलितलौ पादौ कन्यां तां परिवर्जयेत् ।।
येन केनचिदंशेन मांसं यस्या विवर्धते ।
रासभीं तादृशीं विद्यात्र सा कल्याणमर्हति ।।
पादे प्रदेशिनी यस्या अङ्गुष्ठं समतिक्रमेत् ।
दुःशीला दुर्भगा शेया कन्यां तां परिवर्जयेत् ।।
पादे मध्यमिका यस्याः क्षितिं न स्पृशते यदि ।
रमते सा न कौमारे स्वच्छन्दा कामचारिणी ।
पादे अनामिका यस्याः क्षितिं न स्पृशते यदि ।
द्वितीयं पुरूषं हत्वा तृतीये सा प्रतिष्ठिता ।।
पादे कनिष्ठा यस्यास्तु क्षितिं न स्पृशते यदि ।
द्वितीयं पुरूषं हत्वा तृतीये सा प्रतिष्ठिता ।।
न देविका न धनिका न धान्यप्रतिनामिका ।
गुल्मवृक्षसनाम्नी च कन्यां तां परिवर्जयेत् ।।
इन्द्रचन्द्रादिपुरूषसनाम्नी च यदा भवेत् ।
नैताःपतिषु रज्यन्ते याश्च नक्षत्रनामिकाः ।।

आवर्तः पृष्ठतो यस्या नाभिं समनुविन्दति ।
तदपत्यं भवेद्ध्वस्वं स्वायुश्रच विनिर्दिशेत् ।।
पृष्ठावर्ता पतिं हन्ति नाम्यावर्ता पतिव्रता ।
कटघावर्ता तु स्वच्छन्दा न कदाचिद्विरज्यते ।।
यस्यास्तु हसमानाया गण्डे जायेत् कूपकम् ।
रमते सा न कौमारे स्वच्छन्दा कार्यकारिणी ।।
यस्यास्तु गच्छमानायाष्टिट्टीकायति जङ्घिका ।
पुत्रं व्यवस्येत्सा कर्तुं पतित्वे नात्र संशयः ।।
स्थूलपादा च या कन्या सर्वगेषु च लोमशा ।
स्थूलहस्ता च या स्याद्दै दासीं तां निर्दिशेद्बधः ।।
यस्याश्रोत्कटकौ पादौ मुखं च विकृतं भवेत् ।
उत्तरोष्टे च रोमाणि सा क्षिप्रं भक्षयेत्पतिम् ।।
त्रीणि यस्याः प्रलम्बन्ते ललाटमुदरं स्फिचौ ।
त्रीणि भक्षयते सा तु देवरं श्वशुरं पतिम् ।।

Examination of the beauty of a lady could be done on the basis of the beauty and good shape of her hands, feet, fingers, nails, thighs, waist, nose, knees, stomach portion, back, breasts, ears, arms, tongue,, lips, teeth, cheeks, throat, eyes, forehead, head, hair, hair on other body parts, voice, color complexion and navel. A lady having a line or wrinkle on throat and the portion surrounding the eyes being little reddish, brings great progress and prosperity in the family wherever she gets married. One who has the sign of spear in the form of trident on forehead gets a king's destiny and rules over thousands of slaves. A lady who walks like a royal swan or duck and have eyes as well as color complexion like a deer with tooth being symmetrical and glorifying is said to be one of the best. A lady with stomach or visible abdomen's outer part like a frog and appears to be spherical like a banyan tree gives birth to a son who becomes king in future. A girl having a soft voice like duck and color complexion being reddish brown like honey, brings increment in wealth and gives birth to eight sons. Lady with long ears, beautiful well shaped nose and attractive eyebrows like a rainbow gets extreme sensual pleasure. Those who have thin body, wheat color complexion, soft and glorifying body, melodious voice and teeth just like a conch shell or jasmine or shining moon experience ample of wealth. Lady with thick thighs and thin waist like the mid part of an altar with big and broad eyes becomes the wife of a king. Ladies having a mole or a wart at right breast or palm or ear or throat, give birth to boy on their first delivery. A lady, whose glands and veins on the ankle are not visible out of the flesh, fingers very closer to each other, small ankles and attractive waist with reddish colored eyes and soles, experiences gratification in her life. One should not marry with ladies having nails like the back of tortoise, tilted or distorted fingers, and glory less soles. One should consider ladies with excessive increment in flesh of any part of body like a she ass and avoid their company. A lady whose index finger overlaps the thumb of foot is said to be sorrowful and unfortunate for others. A lady whose middle finger of feet does not touch the earth, be virgin before marriage but in future after marriage, she is found to be involved in elicit physical relations with men

46

other than her husband. Whose ring finger of feet does not touch the ground kills her first and second husband and marries the third person. A person should not marry with a girl having the name behind name of deities, grains, animals like elephants or mares, shreds, creepers, thickets and trees. Ladies having the name behind the name of a goddess or stars or with the name resembling to be the name of a man, do not love their husbands. Ladies having a curl of hair on their back or at navel give birth to children who die in the early period of their life. If curl of hair is on the back only then it is problematic and disastrous for husband's life while if it is at the navel of the stomach then such ladies are found to be capricious and utterly self indulgent. Ladies in which dimple appears on the cheeks when they smile, though maintain their chastity in the early period of the life, get involved in illicit sexual relations in future. While walking if a sound resembling the sound of the pronunciation of *tik-tik* is produced in-between the thighs and heel or ankle then such ladies are extremely sexually corrupt and become incest and carry illicit sexual relation even with their sons. A girl having thick foot, hair on the whole body and thick ugly looking hands leads a life of slave. A lady with upper part of the heel being round shaped, stinking mouth because of any incurable disease and hair at upper lips be the cause of death of her husband. Lady whose forehead, stomach and back side of waist are found to be over long becomes the cause of anguish and hazard in the life of her husband, father in law and brother in laws. In the *Agni Puran*, description of a lady on the basis of her physical symptoms is done in the following way:-

शस्ता स्त्री चारुसर्वांगी मत्तमातंगगामिनी ।
गुरूरूजघना या च मत्तपारावतेक्षणा ॥
सुनीलकेशी तन्वंगी विलोमांगी मनोहरा ।
समभूमिस्पृशौ पादौ संहतौ च तथा स्तनौ ।
नाभिः प्रदक्षिणावर्त्ता गुहाम् त्यथत्रवत् गुल्फौ निगूढौ
मध्येन नाभिरंगष्ठमानिका ॥
जठरं न प्रलम्बश्चा रोमरूक्षा न शोभना ।
नर्क्षवृक्षनदीनाम्नी न सदा कलहप्रिया ॥
न लोलुपा न दुर्भाषा शुभा देवादिपूजिता ।
गण्डैर्मधूकपुष्पाभैर्न शिराला न लोमशा ॥
न संहतभ्रूकुटिला पतिप्राणा पतिप्रिया ।

- - - - - - - - -

अलक्षणापि लक्षण्या यत्राकारस्ततो गुणाः ।
भुवडंकनिष्ठिका यस्या न स्पृशेन् मृत्युरेव सा ॥

A lady is said to be worthy in the sense of physical beauty who is well figured and beautiful in every aspect, who walks similar to a exhilarated and boundless elephant, whose thighs and buttocks are heavy and eyes are like the eyes of a intoxicated pigeon, who is having bluish curly hair, slim body with invisible hair on it, who is attractive and marvelous in looking, whose both soles touch the ground equally, breasts are close and touch to each other, whose navel at the stomach is curled towards south or clockwise, whose vagina is like a leaf of *Pipal* tree, whose knees are hidden in the flesh, navel crater is of the size of nail of thumb and stomach is long but not dangling or swinging like a pot belly because of excess flesh. On contrary of this one who is having excess hair on the body thereby making her skin rough is not said to be a virtuous lady. Ladies having similar names to stars, trees and rivers and those who love quarrelling are not said to be commendable. A lady who is altruistic, soft speaking and forgives the mistakes of others is worthy of respect and should be worshipped. A lady having cheeks fair in complexion similar to the flower of the tree *Mahua* or *Bassia Latifolia*, whose nerves are invisible and body is not having visible hair is complimented by people and is auspicious. Lady having tilted eyebrows touching each other at corner is not virtuous. Lady whose husband is her soul and who is very beloved to her husband, is considered to be worthy of respect even if she do not possess any of aforesaid good qualities. Where true beauty resides, there exist propitious qualities. Ladies with last smallest finger of the feet not touching the ground are the symbol of death.

# Internal Architecture of Women

रक्ताश्रयस्तथा श्लेष्माशयः पित्ताशयः परः ।
आमाशयस्तथा पक्वाशयो बाह्याशयो मतः ।।
मूत्राशया इति सप्त प्रोक्तास्ते विप्र भौतिक्ततः ।
पित्तण्क्वाशयान्ते वै स्त्रीणां गर्भाशयोऽष्टमः ।।

Body has seven receptacles termed as arteries or veins, gall bladder, stomach, upper part of alimentary canal, small intestine, large intestine and urinal bladder. Apart of these women have eight receptacle as their womb.

नव स्रोतांसि देहेषु श्रवणे नयने तथा ।।
नासे च वदनं चैव तदा दै गुदशेफसी ।

तानि स्युर्मलवाहानि बहिः सर्ववपुष्मताम् ।।

स्तनयोर्द्वे भगे चैव स्त्रीणां त्रीण्यधिकानि तु ।

Body has nine sources as two ears, two eyes, two nose, mouth, anus and penis. These nine body parts are the shit carriers in all the creatures. In Female, instead of penis, two breasts and vagina exists.

पेशीशतानि वै कञ्च स्त्रीणां विंशाधिका मताः ।
स्तनयोर्दश लक्ष्यन्ते यौवने दश वै भगे ।।
अन्तर्द्वे प्रसृतो बाह्यो तिस्रो वै गर्भ मार्गाः ।
शङ्खनाभ्याकृतिर्योनिस्त्रककयावर्त्यत्र तृतीयके ।।
तस्मिन्नावर्त्तके विप्र गर्भशय्या च संस्थिता ।
रोहितास्या तत्र पेशी शुक्रजीवनिका मता ।।

Generally there are five hundred muscles but in female these are twenty more. They have ten muscles in breast and ten in *Yoni* or vagina. One muscle exists inside the vagina and one outside of it while three at the route of ovary. Vagina in just like the navel of a conch shell and it possess three cycles in the passage. After the third cycle ovary starts. At ovary, the red ended muscle gives life to seminal fluid. During the time of being *Rajaswala* or at the time of menstruating discharge, these three muscles are said to be the dispatcher.

# Nature of Women

A clear description is done regarding the flickering nature of women and their inclination towards sensual pleasure in *Mahabharat* in the colloquy between sage *Nard* and fairy *Panchchuda*. In *Mahabharat* sage *Narad* asks *Panchchuda* about iridescent nature of women which she replied and said "being a lady I can not speak against women". On further request she gives a detailed description of women nature as follows:-

न शक्यामि स्त्री सती निन्दितुं स्त्रिया: ।।
कुलीना रुपवत्यश्चा नाथवत्यश्चा योषित: ।

‒ ‒ ‒ ‒ ‒ ‒ ‒ ‒ ‒ ‒ ‒ ‒ ‒ ‒ ‒

‒ ‒ ‒ ‒ ‒ ‒ ‒ ‒ ‒ ‒ ‒ ‒ ‒ ‒

स्तदैव दोषा: प्रमदासु नारद ।।

Same conversation is described in *Shiv Puran*:-

कुलीना नाथवंत्यश्चा रूपवंतयश्चा योषित: ।।
मर्यादासु न तिष्ठति स दोष: स्त्रीषु नारद ।।
न स्त्रीभ्य: किंचि दन्यद्दै पापीयस्तैरमस्ति हि ।।
स्त्रियो मूलं हि पापानां तथा त्वमपि वेत्थ ह ।।
समाज्ञातानर्थवत: । प्रतिरूपान् यथेप्सितान् ।।
यतीनन्तरमासाद्य नालं नार्य: प्रतीक्षितुम् ।।
असद्धर्मस्त्वयं स्त्रीणामस्मांक भवति प्रभो ।।
पापीयसो नरान् यद्दै लज्जां त्यक्ता भजामहे ।

52

स्त्रियं च यः प्रार्थयते सन्निकर्षे च गच्छति ।।
ईषञ्च कुरुते सेवां तमेवेच्छंति योषितः ।।
नासां कश्चिदमान्योऽस्ति नासां ववसि निश्रचयः ।।
सुरूपं वा कुरूपं वा पुमांसमुपभुंजते ।।
न भयादथ वाक्रोशात्रार्थहेतोः कथंचन ।।
नज्ञातिकुलसम्बन्धस्त्रियस्तिष्ठति भर्तृषु ।।
यौवने वर्तमानानामिष्टाभरणवाससाम् ।।
नारीणां स्वैरवृत्तीनां स्पृहयन्ति कुलस्त्रियः ।।
या हि शश्वच्छह्रु मता रक्ष्यन्ते दयिताः स्त्रियः ।।
अपि ताः सम्प्रसज्जन्ते कुब्जान्धजडवामने ।।
पंगुष्वपि च देवर्षे ये चान्ये कुत्सिता नराः ।।
स्त्रीणामगम्यो लोकेषु नास्ति कश्चिन्महामुने ।।
यदि पुंसा गतिर्ब्रह्मन्कथं चित्रोपपद्यते ।।
अप्यन्योन्यं प्रवर्तन्ते न च तिष्ठन्ति भर्तृषु ।।
अलभात्पुरूषाणां च भयात्परिजनस्य च ।।
वघबन्धभया चैच्च ताभ्रआशा हि योषितः ।।
चलस्वभाव दुश्चेष्टा दुर्गाह्या भवतस्तथा ।।
प्राज्ञस्य पुरूषस्येह यथारतिपरिग्रहात् ।।
नाग्निस्तुष्यति काष्ठानां नापगानां महोदधिः ।।
नान्तकस्सर्वभूतानां न पुंसां वामलोचनाः ।।
इदमन्यच्च देवर्षे रहस्यं सर्वयोषिताम् ।।
दृष्टैव पुरूषं सद्यो योनिः प्रक्लिद्यते स्त्रियाः ।।
सुस्नातं पुरूषं दृष्ट्वा सुगन्धं मलवर्जितम् ।।
योनिः प्र क्लिद्यते स्त्रीणांदृतेः पात्रादिवोदकम् ।।
कायानामपि दातारं कर्त्तारं मान सांत्वयोः ।।
रक्षितारं न मृष्यति भर्तारं परमं स्त्रियः ।।
न कामभोगात्परमात्रालंकारार्थसचयात् ।।
तथा हितं न मन्यन्ते यथा रतिपरिग्रहात् ।।
अन्तकश्शम नो मृत्युः पातालं वडवामुखम् ।।
क्षुरधारा विषं सर्पो वह्निरित्येकतः स्त्रियः ।।

53

Fairy *Panchchuda* describes the nature of women and says that the women who are beautiful, having generous and worthy husband and belong to renowned family even never maintain family's dignity and do not follow the code of conduct. No creature on the earth is more sinful than a woman. Women are the originator and the base of sins as their presence, thoughts and activities give birth to immoral acts. They become unabashed in the passion of love and invite even an abhorred and corrupt man to fulfill their illicit sexual covet. Men get the chance to make a sexual amusement with women only by little care of them and giving them fake compliments. Ladies consider every such man suitable for committing sexual course who is easily available to them. Such ladies who are involved in illicit sexual relations never think of the age, appearance and community of the sexual companion and even do not worry if such man is in their kinship. Women can not be compelled to live in the codes of morality by any kind of fear or intimidations and they never care of the dignity of dynasty or fear of disregard. They can not be controlled even by providing all kind of facilities and wealth. Ladies belonging to renowned families also get influenced by immoral ladies hence inherit the properties of such cunning and sexually corrupt ladies and involve themselves into illicit sexual relations. Ladies of noble families are also found to be involved in adultery during the absence of husbands and do not be indecisive in performing sexual debauchment even with a halt and maimed or a handicapped or an ugly person. If ladies are unable to find the male as companionship then they do artificial mating with each other. Ladies become depressed if they are unable to perform sexual coalition due to the absence of men and fear of family or punishment. It is very difficult for such fickle natured ladies to be husband devotee after marriage. Fire never get satisfied by burning wood and remain hungry, few rivers can not fulfill the thirst of ocean, lord of death is never satisfied to kill numerous creatures similarly no man can fulfill the desires of a woman hence women are always unsatisfied in fulfilling sexual desire and they always remain thirsty even after carrying sexual relations with numerous persons. The moment a lady finds a suitable man, her vaginal liquid or seminal fluid discharges and flows like a water stream coming out from a broken vessel. Ladies do not pay reverence and never obey even those husbands who are of very loving and caring nature for them. For ladies, sex is more important than the wealth, ornaments and self respect. Lord of death, death itself, hell, mare fire or fire beneath the sea, burning fire, poison and snake bite together are not as harmful as a licentious young lady. The above mentioned are the awful qualities which are invoked into a female as she takes birth and they get effective from time to time. In context of behavior of ladies, it is mentioned in the *Mahabharat*:-

एताः कृत्याश्च कार्याश्च भरतर्षभ।
न चैकस्मिन् रमन्त्येताः पुरूषे पाण्डुनन्दन।।
एता हि मनुजव्याघ्र तीक्ष्णास्तीक्ष्णपराक्रमाः।
नासामस्ति प्रियो नाम मैथुने संगमेति यः।।
प्रमदोक्तं तु यत् किंचित् तंत् स्त्रीषु बहु मन्यते।
न तथा मन्यते स्त्रीषु पुरूषो पुरूषोक्तमनिन्दिते।।

Ladies are just like a female witch deity who wants to take away the life of men. When a man is trapped in the snares of illusory world of a woman and accepts her as a fiancée then she finds some other man for love and sexual satisfaction and hence tries to attract some other man. Due to the natural curse of performing illicit mating because of passion for sexual deeds, women keep on changing their male companions and do not stick to a single man. Basically ladies are of rude and shrewd nature though they pretend to be polite and merciful hence they have a gut feeling to commit anything illicit. They never keep affection for a single man because whoever be the partner of them in the mating, be their lover just for that duration. Ladies generally listen and give importance only to the statement spoken by other ladies because of jealousy. As women consider the virtuous qualities of men to be secondary in comparison to their ability to provide sexual relief and wealth hence they do not give importance to the logical sayings of men. According to *Manu Smriti*:-

भिन्दन्त्यवमता मन्त्रं तैर्यग्योनास्तथैव च ।
स्त्रियश्चैव विशेषेण तस्मात्तत्रादृतो भवेत् ।।

If these ladies are dishonored or compelled by their intimate well-wishers for their welfare then also they disclose the secrets of that person to his enemies. Thus one should not involve ladies in the secret discussions. According to

*Brahamm Puran:-* स्त्रीणामेष स्वभावोऽस्ति रतं गोपायितं भवेत् ।

It is the nature of ladies that they want sexual coalition to be done secretly. There is a detailed description of how the depraved qualities are adopted by women and how such women being perilous for men, divert them from the virtuous path, mentioned in religious sayings. According to *Mahabharat*, in context of illusion and infatuation invoked by he presence of women, it is said that:-

एता हि रममाणास्तु वन्चायन्तीह मानवान् ।
न चासां मुच्यते कश्चित पुरुषो हस्तमागतः ।।
गावो नवतृणानीव गृह्नन्त्येता नवं नवम् ।
शम्बरस्य च या माया माया या नमुचेरपि ।।
बलेः कुम्भीनसेश्चैव सर्वास्ता योषितो विदुः ।
हसन्तं प्रहसन्त्येता रुदन्तं प्ररुदन्ति च ।।
अप्रियं प्रियवाक्यैश्च गृह्ते कालयोगतः ।
सम्पूज्यमानाः पुरुषैर्विकुर्वन्ति मनो नृप ।।
अपास्ताश्च तथा राजन् विकुर्वन्ति मनः स्त्रियः ।
न च स्त्रीणां क्रियाः काश्चिदिति धर्मो व्यवस्थितः ।।

निरिन्द्रिया हाशास्ताश्च स्त्रियोऽनृतमिति श्रुति: ।
शय्यासनमलंकारमन्नपानमनार्यताम् ।।
दुर्वाग्भावं रतिं चैव ददौ स्त्रीभ्यः प्रजापतिः ।

Beautiful ladies roaming here and there attract men to deceive them. A man, who keeps propinquity with the women, can never get untouched by the pseudo attraction of the illusory world of them. Young ladies ruin the character and carrier of young boys and devour their virginity just as a cow freely roaming in the ground eats the grass. Ladies are the master of the art of making illusion and are perfect in the techniques of ancient masters of black magic *Shambasur, Namuchi, Bali* and *Kumbhinasi*. Ladies, finding the desired man laughing, themselves laugh with him and on his crying, pretend to be very sad and shed tears with him. They do not know the actual preface or state of mind of themselves. For the sake of sexual satisfaction they pretend false love by cheering and embracing even an ugly person to which they had always kept the feeling of aversion. If ladies are honored by men, they deceive them and make them depressed while if they are insulted by men then they put false blames upon them and prove them guilty in the society. Ladies should stay away from practice of *Vedic Karama* or ultimate scriptural duties. Ladies lack perception or conscience because they do not have control over their senses. They are away from the actual knowledge of religion. God bestowed cot as an indication of laziness, alluring postures, ornaments, variety of delicious

58

foods and grains, shrewdness, love and skill of sexual mating to women as their basic requirements and desires. In *Yagyavalkyopanished*, the awful character of ladies has been described by unclothing the disgusting form of them concealed behind their gorgeous appearance:-

मांसपान्जालिकायास्तु यन्त्रलोकेऽङ्डपन्जारे ।
स्त्राय्वस्थिग्रन्थिशालिन्याः स्त्रियाः किमिव शोभनम् ।।
मेरुश्रृन्गटोल्लासिगगङ्गाजलरयोपमा ।
दृष्टा यस्मिन्मुने मुक्ताहारस्योलासशालिता ।।
श्मशानेषु दिगन्तेषु स एव ललनास्तनः ।
श्रभिरास्वाद्यते काले लघुपिण्ड इवान्धसः ।।
केशकज्जलधारिण्यो दुःस्पर्शा लोचनप्रियाः ।
दृष्कृताग्निशिखा नार्यो दहन्ति तृणवन्नरम् ।।
ज्वलिता अतिदूरेऽपि सरसा अपि नीरसाः ।
स्त्रिया हि नरकाग्रीनामिन्धनं चारु दारूणम् ।।
सर्वेषां दोषरत्नानां सुसमुद्रिकयानया ।
दुःखश्रृङ्खलया नित्यमलमस्तु मम स्त्रिया ।।

This source of attraction, a woman body, is made up of lump of flesh and sources of shit which is like a basket of garbage roaming here and there, contains a mortal body constituting veins, bones and fluid. This woman body is like a hell and is not at all having any kind of attraction for men. The area in-between the breasts of a lady, wearing a necklace around her neck touching her soft breasts, is compared with the water fall at the mountain which appears very beautiful but actually after the death the breast of her body is eaten by dog in funeral house. A lady with beautifully arranged hair, eyes decorated by lampblack, very difficult to get for touching and pleasing to spectator's eyes is actually just like a flame full of awful features and burns the morality as well as character of men to ashes by her lust and misdeeds. Such licentious ladies are like a burning pyre of hell and have the power to divert virtuous men from their right track even from a distance. Thus, may God protect men from the ladies, who are the baskets of all the sins and troubles. This is mentioned in *Brahama Puran* in the following way:-

को नाम लोके राजेन्द्र कामिनीभिर्न वञ्चितः ।
वञ्चकत्वं नृशंसत्वं चञ्चलत्वं कुशीलता ।।
इति स्वाभाविकं यासां ताः कथं सुखहेतवः ।
कालेन को न निहतः कोऽर्थी गौरवमागतः ।।
श्रिया न भ्रामितः को वा योषिद्भिः को न खण्डितः ।
स्वप्नमायोपमा राजन्मदविप्लुतचेतसः ।।
सुखाय योषितः कस्य ज्ञात्वैतद्विज्वरो भव ।

Who is the man in whole universe not ditched by women? Ladies are full of shrewdness, viciousness, shakiness and egotism as these are the fundamental parts of their propensity. Thus, they can never be the cause of real happiness for any one. A man, whose soul is polluted by performing lustful deeds, can never get the ultimate spiritual satisfaction and upright guidance from such deceptive women.

Again, according to the sayings of *Brahama Puran*:-

विषं वृद्धस्य युवती वृद्धाया अमृतं युवा A young girl is just like poison for an old man but a young man is just like the holy water or ambrosia for an old lady. In *Manu Smriti*, the awful character of ladies is explained as following:-

पानं दुर्जनसंसर्गः पत्या च विरहोऽटनम् ।
स्वप्नोऽन्यगेहवासश्च नारीसंदूषणानि षट् ।।
नैता रूपं परीक्षन्ते नासां वयसि संस्थिति: ।
सुरूप वा विरूप वा पुमानित्येव भुञ्जते ।।
पौश्चल्याच्चलचित्ताच्च नैस्नेह्याच्च स्वभावत: ।
रक्षिता यत्नतोऽपीह भर्तृश्चेता विकुर्वते ।।
शय्याऽऽसनमलंकारं कामं क्रोधमनार्जवम् ।
द्रोहभावं कुचर्या च स्त्रीभ्यो मनुरकल्पयत् ।।

- - - - - - - - - -

स्त्रियो ऽनृतमिति स्थित: ।। Ingesting alcoholic beverages, giving preference to the companionship of immoral persons, involving themselves into illicit sexual relations during the absence of husband, unnecessary wandering here and there, enjoying themselves lavishly during famine, staying at other's residences without any proper reason and peeping in to others life are the immoral propensities of ladies. The internal beauty, virtuous qualities and age of a man does not matter to ladies instead the moment they become stimulated by sexual desire, they become ready for sexual coalition just by finding a man. Being *Punschali* or having desire to carry sexual relation with a man other than husband, possessing flickering tendency and always considering sensual pleasure at the top priority in comparison to spiritual or emotional love are the appalling propensities of women making them senseless and because of these, they always harass their husbands by behaving or performing against them even when they are loved and cared by their husbands. Thus for these reasons, according to *Manu Sanhita*, sleeping cots as an indication of excessive luxury or comfort, alluring postures, jewelries, sexual lust, ultimate and unnecessary annoyance, shrewdness, dishonesty, disloyalty and depraved behavior are the appalling properties that could be imagined only for ladies. As ladies are regularly involved in immoral activities and can not speak truth about themselves, hence they mostly speak lie. A shrewd and immodest lady diminishes the noble character of men. According to religious sayings, a man living in the proximity of an immoral lady also gets debauched. According to *SrimadBhagwat Mahapuran:-*

सत्यं शौचं दया मौनं बुद्धिः श्रीर्ह्रीर्यशः क्षमाः ।
शमो दमो भगश्चेति यत्सङ्घात्याति संगयम् ।।
तेष्वशान्तेषु मूढेषु खण्डितात्मस्वसाधुषु ।
संगन कुर्याच्छोच्येषु योषित्क्रीडामृगेषु च ।।
न तथास्य भवेन्मोहो बन्धश्चान्यप्रसंगा ।
योषित्संगाद्यथा पुंसो यथा तत्सङ्गिसंगतः ।।

Ladies whose mere proximity vanishes the truth, sanctity, benevolence, patience, wisdom, prosperity, bashfulness, reputation, mercy feeling and self control, for them, men are mere attractive toys for achieving sexual enjoyment. One should not live in the surrounding of such ladies as well as of the men who have ruined their character with the immediacy of such ladies because nothing in this world is there with which men possess such blind immoral sensual affection as they have with young women.

# Marriage

Different types of women body decorations or cosmetics are mentioned in *Kedar khandam* as:-

श्रृंगाराः षोडश ख्यातास्ताश्च्छृणुष्व महामुने ।
मज्जनं चारू चीरं च तिलकं नेत्ररञ्जनम् ।।
कुण्डलं नासिकामुक्ताफलं कुसुमहारकः ।
केशप्रसाधनं चैव तथा झंकारनूपुरौ ।।
अंगचन्दनलेपश्च कञ्चुकीधारणं तथा ।
कञ्चीकंगणताम्बूलचातुर्यं चेति षोडश ।।

Such adornments applied by women are considered to be of sixteen types and are termed as complete bath, attractive garments, sectarian mark made by saffron or sandal on the forehead as a sign of consecration, lampblack as a cosmetic to eyes, large bangle sized ear ring, nose ring made of gold or silver wire with pearl stick on it, garland of flowers used to adorn hair, hair cosmetics, anklet with bells, smearing with the perfumed paste of sandalwood, beautiful well shaped brassiere or bodice, ornamental belt made up of gold or silver segments, bracelet, betel leaf and alertness or dexterity.

The method by which the ceremony of marriage is done or the way by which the acceptance of bride by bridegroom is done, which is also termed as *Panigrahan*, the marriages are classified in eight types mentioned in *Smrities*. These eight types of marriages are clearly described in *Vishnu Puran* as follows:-

ब्राह्यो दैवस्तथैवार्षः प्राजापत्यस्तथासुरः ।
गान्धर्वराक्षसौ चान्यौ पैशाचश्चाष्टमो मतः ।।

*Braham*, *Dev*, *Aarsh*, *Prajapatya*, *Aasur*, *Gandharv*,
*Rakshasa* and *Pisach* are the eight types of marriages.
Description of these kinds of marriages is done in *Bhawishya*
*Puran* as:-

शुभां लक्षणसम्पन्नां कुलशीलगुणान्विताम् ।
अलङ्कृत्याहिते दानं विवाहो ब्राह्म उच्यते ।।
सहधर्मक्रियाहेतोर्दानं समयबन्धनात् ।
अलङ्कृत्यैव कन्यायाः प्राजापत्यः स उच्यते ।।
प्रदानं यत्र कन्यायाः सहगोमिथुनेन तु ।
सवर्णायाः सगोत्रायास्तमार्षमृषयो विदुः ।।
अन्तर्वेद्यां समानीय कन्यां कनकमण्डिताम् ।
ऋत्विजे चैव यद्दानं विवाहो देवसंज्ञकः ।।
विविक्ते स्वयमयोऽन्यं स्त्रीपुंसोर्यः समागमः ।
प्रीतिहेतुःस गान्धर्वो विवाहः पञ्चमो मतः ।।
हत्वा छित्वा च भित्वा च क्रोशन्तीं रुदतीं गृहात् ।
प्रसह्य कन्याहरणं राक्षसोद्वाह उच्यते ।।
शुल्कं प्रदाय कन्याया हरणं व्यसनादपि ।
प्रसाद हेतुरुक्तोयमासुरः सप्तमस्तथा ।।
सुप्तां मत्तां प्रमत्तां वा रहो यत्रोपगच्छति ।
स पापिष्ठो विवाहानां पैशाचश्चष्टमोऽधमः ।।

If a girl full of auspicious symptoms and virtuous
qualities is married to a worthy man through the religious
process then it is said to be *Braham* Marriage. After finishing
the ritualistic processes, if a girl decorated with ornaments is
bestowed as a blessing to husband then this kind of marriage
is said to be *Prajapatya* marriage. If a marriage is done in the

65

same caste and community and bride is given to bridegroom along with two cows then this kind of marriage is called *Aarsh* marriage. A well decorated girl brought near to the place of fire prepared for religious sacrifice done by a *Pandit* or *Brahmin* and is given to bridegroom as his wife is termed by *Dev* marriage. A love marriage or a marriage where male and female are attracted towards each other either because of infatuation or true love and carry physical relations is said to be *Gandharv* marriage. If a girl unwilling to marry is kidnapped or constrained for marriage by a man of her disliking then such marriage is called *Rakshasa* marriage. Kidnapping or buying a girl at some cost just because of sexual lust and finally pretending it to be a marriage is said to be *Aasur* marriage. Sexually molesting the virginity of a girl by making her to be in excessive sleep or unconsciousness with the help of drugs or alcohol and finally marrying her because of social pressure is said to be *Pisach* marriage.

In *Mahabharat*, *Bhishma* elucidate *Yudhisthara* and says about the five primary types of marriage as *Braham*, *Prajapatya*, *Gandharv*, *Aasur* and *Rakshas*. *Dev* and *Aarsh* kind of marriages are equivalent to Braham marriage and *Pisach* marriage is prohibited like *Rakshas* marriage.

ब्राह्मणानां सतामेष ब्राह्मो धर्मो युधिष्ठिर।

पैशाचश्चासुरश्चैव न कर्तव्यो कथंचन।।

In *Mahabharata*, *Braham*, *Prajapatya*, *Gandharv*, *Aasur* and *Rakshas* marriages are supposed to be the primary types of marriages out of which *Braham*, *Prajapatya* and *Gandharv* marriages are said to be sacred while the other two are against religion. In this way *Braham*, *Dev*, *Aarsh*, *Prajapatya* and *Gandharv* are considered to be the appropriate ways of marriage. The definition of marriage, sexual life and the duties of couple are correlated and explained in religious books. According to *Agni Puran*:-

कन्यादानं शचीयोगो विवाहोऽथ चतुर्थिका ।।

नैकान्तो दोष एकस्त्रियस्तदा केनोपपद्यते ।
धर्मतो यां प्रयच्छन्ति यां च क्रीणन्ति भारत ।।
अन्यैर्गुणैरूपेतं तु शुल्कं याचन्ति बान्धवाः ।
अलंकृत्वा वहस्वेति यो दद्यादनुकूलतः ।।
यन्चा तां च ददत्येव न शुल्क विक्रयो न सः ।
प्रतिगृह्य भवेद् देयमेष धर्मः सनातनः ।।

अनाथां कन्यकां दत्वा नाकलोके महीयते ।।

Marriage constitutes of *Kanyadaan*, *Sachiyoga* or *Matri Puja*, marriage and *Chaturthi Karm*. According to the religious directions, the parents of the girl arrange to organize *Panigrahan* ceremony and give their daughter to bridegroom and from that moment, the whole sole responsibility of taking care of bride becomes of bridegroom. Family members of girl take the money from bridegroom if the bridegroom is less worthy in comparison to the girl, though from that money, they

67

purchase trinkets or other luxury items and donate it to their daughter instead of keeping that with themselves. At the time of marriage, bridegroom gives the precious ornaments to bride. Thus the donation of daughter in *Kanyadaan* done by the parents of bride also constitutes of the ornaments or money given by parents of bride to their daughter and the ornaments given by bridegroom to the parents of bride and this is a very old custom. Hence if someone financially strong contributes in the marriage of an orphan girl or acts as her parents thereby performing *Kanyadaan* of her, is bestowed by utter blessings from God. According to *Mahabharata*:-

स्त्रीधर्मः पूर्व एवायं विवाहे बन्धुभिः कृतः ।
सहधर्मचरी भर्तुर्भवत्यग्निसमीपतः ।।
पाणिग्रहणमन्त्राणां निष्ठा स्यात् सप्तमे पदे ।

पाणिग्रहस्य भार्यास्याद यस्य चाद्धिः प्रदीयते ।
इति देयं वदन्त्यत्र त एनं निश्चयं विदुः ।।

On the occasion of marriage, a girl is directed by her brothers and parents to follow her would be husband and perform the roll of a perfect worthy husband devotee woman after marriage and then she is carried near the sanctified fire where she becomes the wife of a man. At the seventh round or step of *Saptapadi*, the process of marriage completes. The man who takes oath to take care of the lady by taking water in his palm and to whom the lady is donated becomes the husband of that lady. The above is the process of *Kanyadaan*.

68

In this context *Manu Smriti* blesses lady so that her awful qualities may be diminished and she may get prosperity and love of husband. The instructions and blessings for a bride are as follows:-

आशासाना सौमनसं प्रजां सौभाग्यं रथिम् ।
पत्युरनुव्रता भूत्वा सं नह्यस्वामृतायकम् ।।

You should move on the righteous path maintaining your character by following the instructions of a noble husband, always keep good behavior for in-laws, give birth to suitable progeny and bring fortune and wealth in the family.

यथाभिन्दुर्नदीनां साम्राज्यं सुषुवे वृषा ।
एवा त्व सम्राज्येधि पत्युरस्त परेत्य ।।

As the ocean providing us pearls and jewels rules over the rivers in the similar way a virtuous and honest wife should consider herself as a queen in the residence of husband and govern the house as a housewife.

सम्राज्येधि श्वसुरेषु सम्राज्युत देवरेषु ।
ननान्दुः सम्राज्येधि सम्राज्युत श्वश्रवाः ।।

Hey! Virtuous, noble and strong character bride, may you live like the owner of the house in which you should govern your mother in law, father in law, brother in laws and sister in laws to make the integrity of family and to make an amiable environment. In context of man and woman it is said in *Shiv Puran* that:-

तारः पतिश्रुतिर्नारी क्षमा सा स स्वयन्तपः ।।
फलम्पतिः सत्क्रिया सा धन्यौ तौ दम्पती शिवे ।

If wife is the beginning of religious saying then husband is the theme of it, if wife is forgiveness then husband is ascetic fervor or religious austerity which provides that feel of universal sodality to forgive, if wife is a virtuous demeanor then husband is the result of that. Whoever live marital life with this contemplation, are praise worthy. Sexual coalition is defined in the *Brihadaranyak Upnishad* as follows:-

तस्या वेदिरूपस्थो लोमानि बर्हिश्चर्माधिषवणे समिद्धो मध्यतस्तौ मुष्कौ स यावान् ह वै वाजपेयेन यजमानस्य लोको भवति तावानस्य लोको भवति च एवं विद्वानधोपहासं चरत्यासाᳬ स्त्रीणाᳬ सुकृतं वृङ्क्तेऽथ य इदमविद्वानधोपहासं घरत्यस्य स्त्रियः सुकृतं वृञ्जते।।

The genetic organ or vaginal area or *Yoni* of a woman is just like the area of sacrificial fire. The hair on that portion is just like a sitting place made of sacred grass. The flesh of the middle part of it is just like the lower periphery of sacrificial fire. It's middle part is like a burning flame. The adjacent pieces of flesh attached to it at sides are similar like the boundaries of firewood or kindling material for an oblation. Thus the sexual union process when done with spiritual thinking can be compared to *Vajpeya Yagya* and results to virtuous progeny. Keeping such facts in mind when a husband sexually intercourses with his wife, he inherits the virtue of her and if he does not keep the above realization in mind and behave like an insane just to satisfy his sexually yearn then in that case his wife inherits all the upright qualities of him. It is said in *Sastras*:-

भार्यापत्योर्हि सम्बन्धः स्त्रीपुंसोः स्वल्प एव तु।
रति साधारणो धर्म इति चाह स पार्थिवः।।

The mental, spiritual and emotional relation between husband and wife is very strong and beyond imagination while involving themselves into sexual intercourse is a very normal relation because emotional and spiritual affection and feeling gives satisfaction to both of them in this world and after death in next world and the sensual or sexual pleasure is itself hidden in this while the husband-wife relationship based or running over the sensual sexual pleasure, is always proved hell for the husband. After the completion of the marriage ceremony, ladies are blessed in *Atharva Veda* for having a bright future and prosperity as follows:-

सोमस्य जाया प्रथमं गन्धर्वस्तऽपरः पतिः।
तृतीयो अग्निष्टे पतिस्तुरीयस्ते मनुष्यजाः।।
सोमो ददद् गन्धर्वाय गन्धर्वो दददग्नये।
रयिं च पुत्रांश्चादादादग्निर्मह्यमथो इमाम्।।
युवं भगं सं भरतं समृद्धमृतं वदन्तावतोद्येषु।
पतिमस्यै रोक्षक चारू संभलो वदतु वाचमेताम्।।
एषा ने कुलपा राजन् तामु ते परि दहासि।
ज्योक् पितृष्वासाता आ शीर्ण: समीष्यात्।।

A woman purified by sacred verses of *Vedas* married initially with *Soma* or offered to God then she becomes the wife of *Gandharva* or a heavenly minstrel or musician who instructs her to live a melodious way of life. Thirdly *Agni Dev* or God of fire accepts her as his wife and teaches her to struggle in the hard time of the life. Then the fourth husband of her becomes a man who does her *Panigrahan*. It could be said that *Soma* gives the lady to *Gandharv*, *Gandharv* gives the lady to God of fire and finally fire gives her to man who treats her as a wife. It is the duty of her husband to provide her good health, wealth, pleasure and offspring. May husband and wife lead a good life with prosperity and follow the codes of virtuous conduct. Wife should pay reverence to her husband and he should converse to her in pleasant voice. May this bride protect your dynasty and we give her to you so wherever she stays, she shall be happy and spread unity and quietness. Few religions coming after the rise of Hinduism tried to cheat the verses of religious books to mention their new and separate foundations but unfortunately mistook almost religious verses as to aforementioned saying and considered it as a man can marry with four wives at a time. The appropriate behavior of a husband towards his wife is mentioned in *Bhavishya Puran*:-

तस्मात्कार्यमकार्यं वा विज्ञाय प्रभुरागमात् ।
गुणदोषेषु ताः सम्यक्छास्ति राजा प्रजा इव ।।

It is the duty of a husband to extract the right verses and get true knowledge from *Vedas* and behave properly with his wife in a lawful manner watching over her faults and good deeds carefully as a king does with his subjects. In context of married couple's behavior, it has been said through the conversation among *Yudhishthir* and *Bheeshma* in *Mahabharata* that:-

अनृताः स्त्रिय इत्येवं सूत्रकारो व्यवस्यति ।
यदानृताः स्त्रियस्तात सहधर्मः कुतः स्मृतः ।।
अनृता स्त्रिय इत्येचा वेदेष्वपि हि पुज्यते ।
धर्मो ऽयं पूर्विका संका उपचारः क्रियाविधिः ।।
स्वर्गो मृतानां भवति सहधर्मः पितामह ।
पूर्वमेकस्तु म्रियते क चैकस्तिष्ठते वद ।।
श्रुत्वा दम्पतिधर्मे वै सहधर्मे कृतं शुभम् ।
या भवेद् धर्मपरमा नारी भर्तृसमव्रता ।।

*Yudhishthir* presents his doubt in front of *Bhishma* that if ladies tell a lie then how come they are faithful to their husbands and follow the true family duties as telling a lie is an immoral act. How can marital life be righteous if a woman is present in the form of wife? Where goes these marital duties when one of the person dies in a marital couple? Actually if husband and wife together follow the religion only then marital duties are fulfilled in the real sense. The lady who completely follows the religion and code of conduct of married life is the true devotee to husband and is a real life partner. Thus if a wife is having awful propensities or harmful to her husband or his family by any sense then such couple of husband and wife though living together is not performing the actual virtuous obligations of an ideal couple and never blessed by elders, ancestors and God.

# Characteristics Of Bridegroom

It is believed and considered from the beginning that a girl should be married with a suitable person having moral attributes and capable of earning for the necessities. Caressing and cherishing a daughter and marrying her with a worthy man is not a forcefully imposed obligation on parents instead this is a prime duty that can be borne with responsibility by very fortunate parents. The qualities of a worthy bridegroom are described in *Mahabharata* as follows:-

नानिष्टाय प्रदातव्या कन्या इत्यृषिचोदितम् ।
तन्मूलं काममूलस्य प्रजनस्येति मे मतिः ।।
न चैतेभ्यः प्रदातव्या न वोढव्या तथाविधा ।
न द्वेव भार्या क्रेतव्या न विक्रयुया कथंचन ।।

It is a saying of sages that one should not marry his worthy daughter with an unsuitable or undeserving man. If the marriage of a decent girl is done with a suitable and worthy man then only moral attributes could be achieved by the couple thereby providing  them actual sensual pleasure and virtuous progeny. A girl should not be married to a person where it is equivalent to selling her and also one should not marry with such a girl as this is the iniquitous approach of marriage. A girl is not an inanimate object which could be bought or sold. According to *Matsya Puran*:–

वरो दोषाननाख्याय यः कन्यां वरयेदिह।
दत्ताऽप्यदत्ता सा तस्य राज्ञा दण्डयः शतह्रदम्।

If a bridegroom hides his depraved properties and tells a lie about his status to marry a girl then the *Panigrahan* or the process of accepting the bride done by him is considered to be illegitimate and such person is liable for punishment. According to *Brahama Puran-*

श्रीमते विदुषे यूने कुलीनाय यशस्विने।
उदाराय सनाथाय कन्या देया वराय वै।।

One should marry his worthy daughter to a man who is gentle, well educated, young, possessing noble and descent qualities and whose parents are munificent and sympathetic. It is clearly stated in *Sanhita:-*

काममामरणातिष्ठेद् गृहे कन्यर्तुमत्यपि।
न चैवैनां प्रयच्छेतु गुणहीनाय कर्हिचित्।।

It is preferable for a worthy girl to live alone for the whole life without marrying even after being *Ritumati* instead of marrying to a man w

ho is mentally distorted, foolish and with immoral persona.

The above saying is for a worthy and virtuous girl of high moral with no faults in herself. If the girl is not virtuous or having awful qualities or not perfect regarding moral attributes then she should be married by her parents to a man of equivalent characteristics because if such non worthy girl is married to a man of morals then she ruins the life of her husband and the in-laws which is usually found now a days Again physical beauty has nothing to do with internal beauty hence a virtuous girl who is physically unattractive could be married to a worthy man. It is often found in the present scenario that parents marry their morally corrupt daughters of awful behavior to worthy and suitable men by speaking untruth regarding their daughters or by providing plenty of wealth as a bribe in the form of dowry.

# Characteristics of Bride

The selection of a girl for marriage purpose should be done on the basis of her age, beauty, subdivision of caste to which she belongs and virtuous qualities. According to *Manu Smriti*:-

नोद्वहेत्कपिलां कन्यां नाधिकांगी न रोगिणीम् ।
नालोमिकां नातिलोमां न वाचालां न पिंगलाम् ।।
नर्क्षवृक्षनदीनाम्नीं नान्त्यपर्वतनामिकाम् ।
न पक्ष्यहिप्रेष्यनाम्नीं न च भीषणनामिकाम् ।।
अव्यंगांगीं सौम्यनाम्नीं हंसवारणगामिनीम् ।
तनुलोमकेशदशनां मृदंगीमुद्वहेत्स्त्रियम् ।।
यस्यास्तु न भवेद् भ्राता न विज्ञायेत वा पिता ।
नोपयच्छेत तां प्राज्ञः पुत्रिकाधर्मशङ्कया ।।

A person should not marry a girl who possesses brown colored hair, has more body parts than normal case as of more than five fingers on hand or feet, is physically sick and weak, is suffering from incurable disease, having long hair or with no hair on body, is over garrulous and is of yellow colored fainted eyes as all of such symptoms individually indicates to herself being involved in depraved activities. A girl having the name of star, tree, river, *Yaksh*, mountain, bird, snake and a known maid servant's name, should not be chosen for marriage because ladies with such names are destined to be distressed and are of immoral conduct. A lady with no part of her body distorted, having sweet and melodious name, who walks slowly like swan or elephant, having less hairy body, shining hair, small as well as attractive row of teeth and soft skin should be chosen for marriage. A girl who does not have any real brother or whose father in not known by any one should not be considered for marriage because of the possibility of *Putrika Dharm*. The intention of *Putrika Dharm* means having same *Gotra* or exogamous or division of caste group. In other words, an orphan lady of same *Gotra* or lady with no brothers is avoided for choosing as wife because her son also has to perform the funeral or post death sacrificial process for grand parents of mother's side. The other way to understand this saying is, an orphan lady residing in the same community and having no identity regarding family background, may be in blood relation through the chain of ancestors hence being sister could not be considered as being wife. According to *Mahabharat*, a girl worthy for marriage possesses following properties:-

त्रिंशद्वर्षो दशवर्षां भार्यो विन्देत नग्निकाम् ।
एकविंशतिवर्षो वा सप्तवर्षामवाप्नुयात् ॥
यस्यास्तु न भवेद् भ्राता पिता वा भरतर्षभ ।
नोपयच्छेत तां जातु पुत्रिकाधर्मिणी हि सा ॥
असपिण्डा च या मातुरसगोत्रा च या पितुः ॥
इत्येतामनुगच्छेत तं धर्मं मनुरब्रवीत् ॥

A thirty years old man should marry with a girl of the qualities of ten years old who is not a *Rajaswala* or whose menstruations are not started. A man of twenty one years should marry a girl of seven years. As in the present

78

circumstances, a *Kanya* or girl status is obtained by a lady at the age of nine years hence those nine years span is to be added further in the aforementioned age group of marriageable ladies. Hence a man of thirty years should marry with a girl of nineteen years. Again a girl who does not have elder brother and father should not be chosen for marriage because she becomes to be of *Putrika Dharm*. According to *Manu*, a lady who belongs to the same *Pinda* as of a man's mother and does not belong to *Gotra* or same subdivision of a caste of that man's father can be considered for marriage by that man. According to *Smriti*, it is said in the context of *Sapinda* or same *Pinda* that:-

बध्वा वरस्य वा तातः कूटस्थाद यदि सप्तमः ।
पंचमी चेतयोमीता तत्सापिण्ड्यं निवर्तते ।।

*Pinda* means oblation to ancestors. After the seven generations of father and five generation of mother the responsibilities of *Sapind* are over hence one can marry with a girl not directly belonging up to seven generations of father and five generations of mother. The directions of *Markandeya Mahapuran* are as follows:-

व्यंगा विवर्जयेत्कन्यामकुलां चापि रोगिणीम् ।
विकृतां पिंगलां चैव वाचालां सर्वदूषिताम् ।
उद्वहेत्पितृमात्रोश्च सप्तमीं पञ्चमीं तथा ।

A girl even belonging to a renowned and prosperous dynasty also should not be considered for marriage if she is suffering

79

form incurable disease, is handicapped, of malevolent tendencies, mentally retarded, is having yellow-reddish or tawny body complexion and over loquacious. Again a girl who is not related with the seven generations of father and five generation of mother is the right choice for marriage. According *Bhavishya Puran*, following are the properties which a girl should possess while she is selected for marriage:-

नक्षवृक्षनदीनाम्नीं नान्त्यपर्वतनामिकाम् ।
न पश्यहिप्रेष्यनाम्नीं न च भीषणनामिकाम् ।।
अव्यंगांगीं सौम्यनाम्नीं हंसवारणगामिनीम् ।
तनुलोमकेशदशनां मृदंगीमुद्वहेत्रियम् ।।
यस्यास्तु न भवेद् भ्राता न विज्ञायेत वा पिता ।
नोपयच्छेत तां प्राज्ञः पुत्रिकाधर्मशङ्कया ।।

A girl, whose skin is reddish-brown like a monkey, possesses more body parts than the normal count, is always sick because of some incurable disease, having hairless or thick haired body, shrewd natured, yellow-reddish or tawny color complexion and having the name of star-tree-river-mountain-*Yaksh*-snake-servant or a name which can frighten others, is not the right choice for marriage. A girl who does not have a brother and whose father's name is not known, should not be chosen for marriage because by chance she may belong to the same dynasty and may have the relation of sister by previous generations. A girl should have a sweet voice like a swan and her color complexion as well as beauty

80

should match with her would be husband. According to *Vishnu Puran* a girl worthy for marriage should possess the following qualities:-

वपैरेकगुणां भार्यामुद्वहेत्त्रिगुणस्कम् ।
नातिकेशामकेशां वा नातिकृष्णां न पिंगलम् ।।
निसर्गतोऽधिकांगीं वा न्यूनांगीमपि नोद्वहेत् ।
नाविशुद्धां सरोमां वाकुलजां वापि रोगिणीम् ।।
न दुष्टां दुष्टवादयां वा व्यगिनीं पितृमातृतः ।
न श्मश्रुव्यन्चनवर्ती न चैव पुरुषाकृतिम् ।।
न घर्घरस्वरां क्षामां तथा काकस्वरां न च ।
नानिबन्धेक्षणां तद्दृतार्क्षीं नोद्वहेदुधः ।
यस्याश्रच रोमशे जे गुल्फौ यस्यास्तथेत्रतौ ।
गण्डयोः कूपरौ यस्या हसन्त्यास्तां न चोद्वहेत् ।।
नातिरूक्षच्छविं पाण्डुकरजामरूणेक्षणाम् ।
आपीनहस्तपादां च न कन्यामुद्वहेद् बुधः ।
न वामनां नातिदीर्घां नोद्वहेत्संहतभ्रुवम् ।
न चातिच्छिद्रदशनां न करालमुखीं नरः ।।
पन्चमीं मातृपक्षान्चा पितृपक्षान्चा सप्तमीम् ।
गृहस्थश्रोद्वहेत्कन्यां न्यायेन विधिना नृप ।।

A man should marry a girl who is one third of his age. Again nine years span is to be added further in the age of girls. Hence a man of twenty one years should marry a girl of seven plus nine that is sixteen years. This kind of calculation done to achieve the marriageable age group of a girl by adding the nine years in the age calculated from the age of her would be bridegroom is done only when the bridegroom has achieved the age of eighteen years. If a man of the age group of below eighteen is married then his spouse should be seven years younger to him. A girl with more or less hair on the body and very dark or wheat colored complexion in comparison, is not worthy to select for marriage. A girl who possesses more or less body parts by birth or who is not physically pure because of keeping illicit sexual relations or who carries incurable disease or whose family does not stand economically or legendarily in comparison to the dynasty of bridegroom, is not worthy for marriage. A noble man having prudence and conscience, should not marry a girl who is of very shrewd nature, harsh speaking, not keeping the dignity of the family, having the sign of moustaches, possessing man like nature and body figure, having the distorted unpleasant voice like a crow and having round shaped eyes. A girl having hairy thighs and cheeks with over deep dimples should not be considered for marriage. A man should not keep any relation with a girl having extreme inglorious face appearing to be ill-omened, yellowish-white or pale colored nails, reddish eyes or the one who possesses very thick hands and legs. Girl who is of very short or long height, who has both eyebrows joint at the corner, having space between teeth or have distorted teeth coming out of the lips, should not be considered for marriage. A girl who does not have any relation with five generations of mother and seven generations of father is applicable for marriage. According to *Agni Puran*, the measurement of selection of a girl for marriage purpose is done in the following ways:-

विवाहः सदृशैस्तेषां नोत्तमैर्नाधमैस्तथा।
नैकगोत्रां तु वरयेत्रैकार्षेयां च भार्गव।
पितृतः सप्तमादूर्ध्वं मातृतः पश्चामात्तथा।।

Marriage should be done in the family of equivalent economic and social standard and same community. It should not be done in a comparatively very low standard or a very high standard family. A girl who belongs to the same *Gotra* or the same subdivision of community should not be selected for marriage. Again a girl who does not have any relation with the above five generations of mother and seven of father is appropriate for wedlock.

# Freedom of Women

Ladies as daughters, wives and sisters, should be strictly kept under discipline by men but a man has no right to order or compel his mother to be in discipline. There is a clear description in religious sacred scriptures whether ladies should get full freedom or not. It has been found in the examples happening in the society from history till present that women who behave freely and are not controlled by men become of illicit character because of basic lack of restraint in them. It is mentioned in *Mahabharat*, that an old lady invited sage *Astawakra* for sexual intercourse stating that she was unrestrained because of being unmarried. *Astawakra* says that:-

स्वतन्त्रा त्वं कथं भद्रे ब्रूहि कारणमत्र वै।
नास्ति त्रिलोके स्त्री काचिद् या वै स्वातन्त्रकयमर्हति।।
पिता रक्षति कौमार्ये भर्ता रक्षति यौवने।
पुत्राश्च स्थाविरे काले नास्ति स्त्रीणां स्वतन्त्रता।।

None of the lady in all three worlds is worthy to get freedom. At the time of adolescence, father protects her, after marriage husband protects her and at the time of old age, she is looked after by son. Thus liberty is not meant for ladies. According to *Manu Smriti*:-

बालया व युवत्या व वृद्धया वाऽपि योषिता ।
न स्वातन्त्र्केयेण कर्तव्यं किश्चित्कार्यं गृहेष्वपि ।।
बाल्ये पितुर्वशे तिष्ठेत्पाणिग्राहस्य यौवने ।
पुत्राणां भर्तरि प्रेते न भजेत्स्त्री स्वतन्त्रताम् ।।
पित्रा भर्त्रा सुतैवापि नेच्छेद्विरहमात्मनः ।
एषां हि विरहेण स्त्री गर्हो कुर्यादुभे कुले ।।
अस्वतन्त्राः स्त्रियः कार्याः पुरूषैः स्वैर्दिवानिशम् ।
विषयेषु च सज्जन्त्यः संस्थाप्या आत्मनो वशे ।।

Whether a female is a small girl or adolescent or an aged lady, she should not work independently because she lacks discretion. A lady in her childhood should learn the difference between upright and iniquitous deeds, living under the patronage of father. In adolescence after marriage, she should follow the path shown by a righteous husband. In old age or after the death of husband, she should live under the social and economical shelter of sons. Thus ladies should accept the help and patronage of parents or husband or sons thereby not allowing themselves to live freely and involving in illicit sexual relations. A lady not living with parents or husband or sons curses the families of both father and husband because such ladies are usually found to be involved in harlotry. Husband should never give full freedom to their wives and should keep an eye on their activities. For ladies, freedom is the first step of tending towards illicit sexual relations. If a wife is beautiful, lusty and has excessive amorous desires then she should be controlled very strictly by husband.

# Protection of Women

The meaning of protection of women is to protect them from the side effects of their own lust. Though it is mentioned in the ancient scriptures that it's impossible to keep women protected from committing sins and from their excessive lust still it is believed that proper guidance and control done by men on ladies and their own strong determination can keep them away from performing illicit sexual coalition and immoral conduct. In *Mahabharath*, such kind of matters and doubts regarding the protection of women are described as follows:-

अनृतं सत्यमित्याहुः सत्यं चापि तथानृतम् ।

इति यास्ताः कथं वीर संरक्ष्याः पुरुषैरिह ।

वाचा च वधबन्धैर्वी क्लेशैच अविधैस्तथा ।।

न शक्या रक्षितुं नार्यस्ता संयता ।।

The ladies, who always tell lies, cannot be protected or stopped by men from committing social sexual crime. A lady can not be sheltered through apposite supervision or fear of punishment or by keeping her in confinement or captivity because she does not possess self-control over her longing for sexual pleasure. According to *Manu Smriti*:-

न कश्रिचद्योषित: शक्त : प्रसह्य परिरक्षितुम् ।

अर्थस्य संग्रहे चैनां व्यये चैवं नियोजयेत् ।

शौचे धर्मेऽत्रपक्तयां च परिणाह्मस्य वेक्षणे ।

अरक्षिता गृहे रूद्धा: पुरूषैराप्तकारिभि: ।
आत्मानमात्मना यास्तु रक्षेयुस्ताः सुरक्षिताः ।।

It is impossible to protect ladies by punishment or by any kind of compulsion because they wear the mask of bashfulness but actually are of unabashed nature. A lady should be kept busy on subjects like expenditure on homely items, cleaning house, kitchen and religious rituals. Ladies, even when protected by elders and forcefully kept at home, are found to be involved in illicit sexual relations because of lack of restraint in them and their abandoned tendency. Only those ladies, who have self-control over their excessive craving for sexual relations, can maintain their chastity. The ways to protect ladies are in detail described in *Bhavishya Puran*:-

स्वाश्रयेण विना शक्यं न यस्माद्रक्षणादिकम् ।

हेतवो हि त्रिवर्गस्य विपरीतास्तु मानद ।
अरक्षणाद्विवन्त्यस्मादमीषां रक्षणं मतम् ।।
निसर्गातुंर्स्यसन्तोषादुगुणदोषविमर्षतः ।
दुष्टानां चापि संसर्गाद्रिख्या एव च योषितः ।।

पुरुषस्थानवेश्मानि त्रिविधं प्राहुराश्रयम् ।

---

विभक्तयनोद्देशमाप्तवृद्धैरधिष्ठितम् ।।
अरक्षणाद्धि दाराणां वर्णसङ्करजादयः ।
दृष्टा हि बहवो दोषास्तस्माद्रक्ष्याः सदा स्त्रियः ।।
न ह्यासां प्रमदं दद्यात्र स्वातन्त्र्यं न विश्वसेत् ।
विश्वस्तवच्च चेष्टेत न्याय्यं भर्त्सनमाचरेत् ।।
नाधिकारं क्वचिद्दद्यादृते पाकादिकर्मणः ।
स्त्रीणां ग्रामीणवत्ता हि भोगायालं सुशासिता ।।
नित्यं तत्कर्मयोगेन ताः कर्तव्या निरन्तराः ।
इत्येवं सर्वदा व्याप्तेः स्यादविद्यानिराश्रया ।।

..............................

पानाशनकथागोष्ठीप्रियत्वाकर्मशीलता ।।
कुहकेक्षणिकामुण्डाभिक्षुकीसूतिकादिभिः ।
गोप्रसङैस्तथा  सद्विलङ्गियाचकशिल्पिभिः ।।
संवाहोद्यानयात्रासृद्यानेष्वामन्त्रणादिषु ।
प्रसङैस्तीर्थयात्रार्थं धर्मेषु प्रकटेषु च ।।
विप्रयोगः सदा भर्त्रा तज्ज्ञातिकुलनिःस्वता ।
अमाधुर्यकदर्यत्वे भृशं पुंसां च वाच्यता ।।
अतिक्रौर्यमतिक्षान्तिरत्यन्ताभीतिपातनम् ।
स्त्रीभिर्जितत्वमत्यर्थं सत्यं तास्ताः सदोषताः ।
स्त्रीणां पत्युरधीनत्वात्सुमानेव हि निन्द्यते ।
भर्तुरिव हि तज्जाड्यं यद् भृत्यानामयोग्यता ।।
तस्माद्यथोदितास्वेता रक्ष्याः शासनताडनैः ।
ताडनैश्च यथाकालं यथावत्समुपाचरेत् ।।
परिगृह्य बहून्दारानुपचारैः समो भवेत् ।
यथाक्रमोचितैः कर्म दानसत्कारवासनैः ।
प्रथमोऽभिजनो धर्मो योग्यत्वं च सुपुत्रता ।

पक्षे वित्तं विशेत्त्रीणां मानस्तत्कारणं तथा ।।
तस्मान्मानो न कर्तव्यो हेयश्चापि न तत्कृतः ।
गुरूत्वे लाघवे वापि सतां कार्यं निबन्धनम् ।।
तस्मात्सुरक्षिता नित्यमुपचार्येर्यथोचितैः ।
सुभृतां नित्यकर्माणः कर्तव्या योषितः सदा ।
उत्तमां सामदानाभ्यां तु मध्यमाभ्यां ।
पश्चिमाभ्यामुभाभ्यां च अधमां सम्प्रसाधयेत् ।।
भेददण्डौ प्रयुज्यापि प्रागपत्याद्यपेक्षया ।
तच्छिष्टानां तदा पश्चात्सामदानप्रसाधने ।
यास्तु विध्वस्तचारित्रा भर्तुश्चाहितकारिकाः ।
त्याज्या एवं स्त्रियः सद्धि कालकूटविषोपमाः ।।

The protection of the ladies can not be done without strict security and shelter provided by men in the same way as the protection of money. Ladies are very obliging in achieving sensual pleasure, in the practice of religion and in saving the wealth but due to lack of proper control over them, they vanish all of these three indispensable requirements. Ladies should be vehemently kept in discipline. Ladies should be protected from their propensity of dwelling here and there, indecisive and immodest predisposition, all fundamental shortcoming of their nature, tendency of always being disgruntled even when all the possible amenities are granted to them and from the enthusiasm for the immediacy of nefarious and sexually corrupt persons. Socially appointed men for the protection of ladies as husband, father and brother, proper place for dwelling and their own residence are considered to be tenable destination for ladies. The bedroom of ladies should be located at secure place and isolated from other rooms. Ladies should be sheltered under the supervision and control of virtuous and morally strong elders. If the ladies are not strictly controlled and watched then they give rise to the generation of cross-breeds as they commit illicit sexual mating with other men and get pregnant, lying to their husbands that the child is of them.

One should not provide intoxicant items like drugs or wine, raw meat and indecent literature to ladies. They should never been given complete freedom and their statements shouldn't be trusted blindly. One should behave properly and trust his wife but timely should menace on her wrong deeds. A lady, following the code of conduct, should be given household jobs and should also be given the opportunity to get skilled in this. Ladies should always be kept busy in household works and should not allow sitting idle. They should be respected but should be kept in control by the fear of punishments. The first quality of ladies is to be devoted towards family duties, after this, involvement in rituals and giving birth to children are their other qualities.

A lady with appreciable character should be made happy and in-control by pleasant talks, gifts in the form of jewelries or money and praises. A lady with medium qualities should be made delighted and under control by providing her jewelries, money and by fear of punishments. A lady of wicked or despicable temperament should be controlled by terror and punishments. Initially such nasty minded ladies should be chastised either verbally or physically and after the birth of child they should be controlled by proper guidance or by bribe in the form of jewelries, money etc. otherwise they start instructing immoral doings to children. Ladies, who are utterly iniquitous and cruel, are like fatal poison which exterminates the life of husbands in seconds. Such ladies are very treacherous hence should be isolated and divorced immediately.

# Duties of Married Women

Description of the duties of a husband devotee wife is done in *Mahabharat* in the following way:-

शुश्रूषां परिचारं च देवतुल्य प्रकुर्वती ।

वश्या भावेन सुमनाः सुव्रता सुखदर्शना ।
अनन्यचित्त सुमुखी भर्तुः सा धर्मचारिणी ।।
परुषाण्यपि चोक्ता या दृष्टा दुष्टेन चक्षुषा ।
सुप्रसन्नमुखी भर्तुर्या नारी सा पतिव्रता ।।

The lady who respects her worthy husband and considers him to be having whole of her possession because of the natural love for him, who do not let shade of grief to influence her, keeps caring for her husband, performs religious observances for the augmentation of the health, age and affluence of the husband by collaborating him in rituals, decorates herself to be attractive for her husband, who is not attracted towards other men and who, when menaced by the husband on a misdeed, hears very patiently and accepts her mistake, is said to be a husband devotee. Ladies have been directed in *Harivansh Puran* accordingly:-

दानोपवासपुण्यानि सुकृतान्यप्यरुन्धति ।
निष्फलान्यसतीनांहिपुण्यकानितथाशुभे ।।
या वन्चान्ति भर्तारं योनिदुष्टाश्रच याः स्त्रियः ।
योनिदोषात् पुण्यफलं नाश्नन्ति निरयंगमाः ।।

अवाग्दुष्टाः शौचयुत्ता धृतिमत्यः शुभव्रताः ।
सततं साधुवादिन्यो धारयन्ति जगत् खलु ॥
योनिदुष्टस्त्रियो नास्ति प्रायश्चितं हतैव सा ।
कल्पान्तरसहस्रेषु न स्त्री सा लभते गतिम् ।
तिर्यग्योनिसहस्रेषु पच्यते योनिविप्लवात् ॥
भर्ता देवः सदा स्त्रीणां सद्विर्दृष्टस्तपोधने ।
यस्या हि तुष्यते भर्ता सा सती धर्मचारिणी ॥
कौतूहलहतानां तु स्त्रीणां लोको न शोभनः ।
अश्रुप्रपातो रोषश्चच कलहश्चच कृतः सति ।
उपवासाद् व्रताद् वापि सद्यो भ्रंशयति स्त्रियः ॥
या शेषभोजिनी नित्यं नैव च स्यादरून्तुदा ।
न च स्याद् व्यशना सौम्ये नित्यं च पतिदेवता ॥
शौचान्विता च सततं न च रूक्षाभिभाषिणी ।
श्वश्रूश्वशुरयोर्नित्यं शुश्रूषाभिरता सती ॥
किं तस्या व्रतकैः कार्यं किं वा स्यादुपवासकैः ।

The outcome of the charity, pray service and meditation, done by ladies who tell lies and are not of virtuous conduct, go in vain. Ladies, who cheat their husbands, break their trust by being disloyal to them and whose virginity or chastity is ruined because of illicit sexual relations or *Yoni* is polluted because of committing harlotry, are send to hell after death. Those who are having patience, speak gently, never scold others, never criticize others in their absence, speak truth and do not keep illicit sexual relations, seek the ultimate happiness in this world and in the other world. There is no way to repent for the women who pollute their *Yoni* or vagina by involving themselves into illicit sexual relations. Such kinds of ladies take birth in thousands of *Yonis* or incarnations after death and in every such re-embodiment, they have to endure ultimate agony and never become free from the punishment for the transgression of committing adultery. For women, their individual morally high husband is like a God. Ladies who behave and obey according to a righteous husband are said to be the true followers of the religion. A lady, who sexually intercourses with a man other than her husband because of curiosity or her excessive sexual lust, occupies hell after death. The howling or lamenting acrimoniously, quarrelling and adultery done by a lady, vanishes the auspicious outcome of all the virtuous deeds done by her parents or husband. A lady, who eats after feeding every one at house, never hurts another's sentiments by harsh speaking or rude behaviour, does not show her annoyance by hunger strike, always behaves as a husband devotee, follows the codes of demeanor and purity and obeys her in-laws, need not worry for worshiping God. The obligations and special guidelines for ladies mentioned in *Bhavishya Puran* are the following:-

हीनोऽन्यः शासनीयस्तु तत्र तावन्न विद्यते ।
योग्यता सुतसौभाग्यैन यावत्स्यात्प्रतिष्ठिता ।।
देवरैः पतिमित्रैश्च पहिसक्रियोचितैः ।
विविक्तदेशावस्थान वर्जयेदिति नर्म च ।।
प्रायशो हि कुलस्त्रीणां शीलविध्वंसहेतवः ।
दुष्टयोगो रहो नित्यं स्वातन्त्र्यमतिनर्मता ।।

दृष्टसंगे त्वरा स्त्रीणां युवभिर्नर्म नोचितम् ।
निर्भेषता स्वतन्त्राणां साफल्यं रहसि व्रजेत् ॥
पुंसो दुष्टेंगिताकारान्दुष्टभावप्रयोजितान् ।
भ्रातृवत्पितृवच्चैतान्पश्यती परिवर्जयेत् ॥
पुंसो न्याग्रहमालापस्मितविप्रेक्षितानि च ।
करान्तरेण द्रव्याणां निबन्धं ग्रहणार्पणम् ॥
द्वारप्रदेशावस्थानं राजमार्गावलोकनम् ।
प्रेक्षोद्यानादिशीलत्वं निरूध्यादुदेशमालयम् ॥
बहूनां दर्शने स्थानं दृष्टिवाक्कायचापलम् ।
ष्ठीवनत्वं ससीत्कारमुच्चैर्हसितजल्पितम् ॥
सांगत्यं लिंगिदुष्टस्त्रीभिक्षुणीकादिभिः ।
मन्त्रमण्डलदीक्षायां संगिः संवसनेषु च ॥
इत्येवमादिदुर्वृत्तं प्रायोदुष्टजनोचितम् ।
वर्जयेत्परिरक्षन्ती कुलत्रितयवाच्यताम् ॥
हिंदोलकादिक्रीडायां प्रसक्तां तरुणीं निशि ।
रममाणां विटैः सार्धं विधवां स्वैरचारिणीम् ॥
वृद्धादिभार्यां सज्जायां यान्गेयादिसंगिनीम् ।
कः श्रद्दध्यात्सतीत्येवं साध्वीमपि हि योषितम् ॥
पातयन्त्येव दौःशील्यादात्मानं सकुलोत्रयम् ।
उद्धरन्ति तदैवैताः स्त्रियश्चरित्रभूषणाः ॥
सम्बाधानां प्रदेशानां नित्यं स्वेदादिमार्जनम् ।
दन्तनासादिपङ्कानां विगन्धस्य च शोधनम् ॥
न कापि दुर्भगा नाम सुभगा नाम जातितः ।
व्यवहाराद्भवत्येष निर्देशो रिपुमित्रवत् ॥

A bride is not supposed to be making her opinion to put upon others or to preside over the house of her husband, till she gives birth to a child. A noble lady should not halt or gossip in a secluded place with her brother-in-laws or friends of husband because it obliterates the virtuousness or disposition of her. A bride should not accompany herself with scoundrel people and should not joke with men other than husband. Malicious sexual attempt to seduce a man in a secluded place, done by a capricious natured or freedom loving unrestrained lady, always succeeds. A lady should avoid and entirely ignore the indecent signs, gestures, comments and behavior passed by an adulterer man. The behavior or activities forbidden for a noble lady are unnecessary joking with men other than husband, exchanging items or money in order to achieve sexual pleasure by touching other men, standing on the door without any reason, sitting for long duration on window or on a lattice window and gazing towards the road, walking in gardens without the presence or consent of a man who is morally authorized to take care of her like husband, having capriciousness of eyes, voice and body, spitting here and there with sound, laughing deafeningly, unnecessary and worthless conversations, speaking ill of others in their absence and accompanying sages, beggars or wicked ladies. If a lady is interested in swinging on a cradle or playing outdoor games during the night time or likes the company of jesters and unabashed people or involved in sexual debauchment even after being a widow or a young lady married to an old man shows her sensual affection towards illegitimate sexual relations and music of buffoons, then she can not be considered as a noble lady. A lady of immoral conduct acts as a black sheep of the family and destroys all three dynasties including ancestors of the family of her father and husband and the forthcoming descendants, by producing crossbreeds because of their immoral character while they vanishes all the sins of above mentioned three dynasties if they are of virtuous and moral character. Ladies should keep their stomach, buttocks and genital organs clean and pure as they give birth to progenies and this is the only reason that they are worthy to be worshipped. No lady is fortunate or unfortunate by birth instead it is her behavior and character, which imparts such destiny. According to *Manu Sanhita*:-

सन्तुष्टो भार्यया भर्ता भर्त्रा भार्या तथैव च।
यस्मिन्नेव कुले नित्यं कल्याणं तत्र वै ध्रुवम् ।।
विशीलः कामवृत्तो वा गुणैर्वा परिवर्जितः ।
उपचर्यः स्त्रिया साध्या सततं देववत्पतिः ।।
नास्ति स्त्रीणां पृथग्यज्ञो न व्रतं नाप्युपोषणम् ।
पतिं शुश्रूषते येन तेन स्वर्गे महीयते ।।
कामं तु क्षपयेद्देहं पुष्पमूलफलैः शुभैः ।
न तु नामापि गृहीयात्पत्यौ प्रेते परस्य तु ।।
आसीतामरणात्क्षान्ता नियता ब्रह्मचारिणी ।
यो धर्म एकपत्नीनां काङ्क्षन्ती तमनुत्तमम् ।।
पतिं हित्वाऽपकृष्टं स्वमुत्कृष्टं या निषेवते ।
निन्द्यैव सा भवेल्लोके परपूर्वेति चोच्यते ।।
स्त्रीणां साक्ष्यं स्त्रियः
प्रजनार्थं महाभागाः पूजार्हा गृहदीप्तयः ।
स्त्रियः श्रियश्च गेहेषु न विशेषोऽस्ति कश्चन ।।

97

If a lady's husband is trapped by the infatuation of an other lady, then she should not leave her husband finding herself unappealing to him in comparison to that lady instead she should try to set her husband free from the snares of the sexual fascination created by that other lady because it is the mistake of that lady not of her husband. There are no special customs and rituals for ladies because they can attain the ultimate happiness on earth and on the other world after death, by following their virtuous husbands. A widow should consume vegetarian food and should stop taking wine or non-vegetarian items. She should not involve herself in earning money through illicit sexual relations and should not sexually pollute the society and young boys. Perhaps to perform this, she may suffer financial problems and possibly not get sufficient meal thereby may become physically thin and lean. If a widow wants to continue her husband devotee religion then she should not involve herself into adultery. If a lady chooses some other man for herself due to the incapability of her virtuous husband to provide sensual pleasure as wealth and other luxuries then she is an adulteress. There should be female witnesses in the judiciary matters against ladies because if there would be a male person instead of female, ladies could motivate him to tell a lie by utilizing their sexual appeal. Ladies are worthy of respect only because they give birth to progenies. Thus they are praiseworthy only in the role of a mother and are said to be queen of the house because it is assumed that they are of virtuous and moral conduct. According to *Srimadbhagwat Mahapuran*:-

स्त्रीणां च पतिदेवानां तच्छुश्रूषानुकूलता ।
तद्बन्धुष्वनुवृत्तिश्च नित्यं तदुत्तधारणम् ।।
संमार्जनोपलेपाभ्यां गृहमण्डलवर्तनैः ।
स्वयं च मण्डिता नित्यं परिमृष्टपरिच्छदा ।।
कामैरुन्चावचैः साध्वी प्रश्रयेण दमेन च ।
वाक्यैःसत्यैः प्रियैः प्रेम्णा काले काले भजेत् पतिम् ।।
संतुष्टालोलुपा दक्षा धर्मज्ञा प्रियसत्यवाक् ।
अप्रमत्ता शुचिः स्निग्धा पतिं त्वपतितं भजेत् ।।

A lady who cares for her husband, obeys him, respects his relatives and protects herself from her sexual craving for men other than her husband, is considered to be a husband devotee and this is the only religion of a married lady. A virtuous lady is the one who keeps unadulterated her house as well as herself. The one, who respects her husband, keeps courteous disposition, controls over her senses, speaks gently and never tells a lie is worthy of respect. It is necessary for a noble lady to possess satisfying nature, generosity, nimbleness, devoutness, knowledge and submissiveness. If a husband is of virtuous character and is not involved in illegitimate sexual relations then a wife should give him the permission for sexual mating with her on his demand.

तुष्टे भर्तरि नारीणां तुष्टाः स्युः सर्वदेवताः ।
विपर्यये तु नारीणामवश्यं नाशमान्नुयात् ।।

A lady is ever blessed by the God if her husband is satisfied by the upright nature of her. If a husband is not happy because of the licentious performance of his wife, then on earth she may continue with her debauched propensity and awful activities but she shall be chastised in the hell after her demise. It is mentioned in *Mahabharat* that ladies should not consider the rumors and misapprehensions as truth that men are responsible for their deprived condition because if a lady is tormented mentally or physically then such harassment of her is only done by other ladies not by men.

स्त्रियश्चैव विशेषेण स्त्रीजनस्य गतिः परा ।
गौर्यो गच्छति सुश्रोणि लोकेऽवेषा गतिः सदा ॥

Ladies are the ultimate destiny of ladies. The humiliation, degradation or harassment of a lady is done by other ladies. Any kind of physical, sexual, mental or social harassment of women has nothing to do with men. This is frequently seen in this world.

It is often found that a worthy and noble lady is also blamed and few ladies after being *Sati* are scolded by other ladies. The only reason behind this is, at present, almost women have no ideals and character hence being involved in sexual debauchery, they scold every righteous women, which are so less in population that can be counted on fingers. Blaming a *Sati* woman or a righteous woman by other sexually corrupt women is just like an attempt done by women to spit on moon. Such type of blames gives rise to public censure. According to *Bhavishya Puran*:-

तस्माद्यथोक्तमाचारमनुतिष्ठेत्सुसंयता ।
मिथ्यालग्नेऽप्यसद्वादः कम्पयत्येव तत्कुलम् ।
प्रियापि साधुवृत्तापि विख्याताभिजनापि च ।
जनापवादात्सम्प्राप सीतानर्थं सुदारुणम् ।।

A bride, belonging to a noble family, should strictly follow the codes of virtuous conduct peacefully because a false blame put on even a *Sati* or virtuous lady ruins the honor of her family. Deity *Sita*, belonging to very high dynasty and being very dear to her husband lord *Ram*, also had to go through the public menace due to fictitious accuses put on her because of rumors spread by ladies.

It is mentioned in *Mahabharat*, that after the assassination of the king *Rawan*, *Sita* had to go through the *Agni Pariksha* thereby proving herself to be chaste because she was kidnapped by *Rawan* and bound to live under his custody for few days. Sri *Ram* set *Sita* free from the relation of wedlock due to rumors spread in public. After the assassination of *Rawan*, Sri *Ram* said to his wife *Sita*:-

कथं हास्यद्विघो जातु जानन् धर्मविनिश्चयम् ।
परहस्तगतां नारीं मुहूर्तमपि धारयेत् ।

"According to the customs of the religion, no man shall accept his own wife who has been kidnapped or take away by other man". In this matter *Sita* accepts the statement said by

Sri *Ram* as the order given to her by her husband but *Laxman* tried to resist him in a polite way. *Sita* knew that she has committed the unpardonable mistake. She disobeyed lord *Ram*'s directions and put the false blame of being characterless on *Laxman*, who was just guarding her on exile on the directions of his elder brother lord *Ram*. This was a serious and unforgivable offence and this became the reason of abduction of *Sita* because *Laxman* left her when she blamed on his character. Though in present environment when an immoral and sexually corrupt wife falsely blames the relatives of her husband then the husband trusts her and breaks the relationship with innocent parents and other relatives in blind affection of his wife. Ladies, who are crossbreeds or who involve in adultery and the people of false religions, very easily question on the morality of decision taken by lord *Ram* and try to prove it wrong.

# Woman in the Role of Mother

Ladies, in the role of mother, are said to be very respective and praiseworthy and this is mentioned in *Brahama Puran* as follows:-

मातृस्तु गौरवादन्ये पितृनन्ये तु मेनिरे।

दुष्करं कुरुते माता विवर्धयति या प्रजाः।

सर्वेषामेव शापनां प्रतिघातो हि विद्यते।
न तु मात्राभिशप्तानां क्वचिच्छापनिवर्त्तनम्॥

न हि मातृसमो बन्धुर्जन्तूनामस्ति भूतले॥

मातृदोषेण वेश्येरितमतिस्त्वभूत्॥

The roll of mother is more glorious than father, in this regard there are different opinions but it is true that the mother who provides proper guidance to her children and takes care of them with sincerity is more respectable comparatively to father. A person can get rid of any curse in the world but it is impossible for him to get rid of a curse given to him by his mother. No body on this earth is more trustworthy for a person than his mother. If a mother is involved in sexual debauchery then her daughters also do the same.

# Instructions to Men

The men and women were given strict directions and guidelines by the religion to live an abstemious and principled life. Though it appears to be very hard to pursue the ancient ethical views in today's life but this is also true that in past, the period when such rules were strictly followed, the society would have the strong social arrangements and people would be leading their life in a teetotal way with full of moral attributes. According to *Manu Smriti-*:

मात्रा स्वस्रा दुहित्रावा न विविक्तसनो भवेत्।
बलवानिन्द्रियग्रामो। विद्वांसमपि कर्षति।।
अविद्वांसमलं लोके विद्वांसमपि वा पुनः।
प्रमदा ह्यत्पथं नेतुं। कामक्रोधवशानुगम्।।
शोचन्ति जामयो यत्र विनश्यत्याशु तत्कुलम्।
न शोचन्ति तु यत्रैता वर्धते तद्धिसर्वदा।।
सुवासिनीः कुमारीश्रच रोगिणो गर्भिणीः स्त्रियः।
अतिथिभ्योऽग्र एवैतान्भोजयेदविचारयन्।।
रजसाऽभिप्लुतां नारीं नरस्य ह्युपगच्छतः।
प्रज्ञा तेजो बलं चक्षुरायुश्चैव प्रहीयते।।
तां विवर्जयतस्तस्य रजसा समभिप्लुताम्।
प्रज्ञा तेजो बलं चक्षुरायुश्चैव प्रवर्धते।।
नाश्नीयाद्धार्यया सार्धं नैनामीक्षेत चाश्नतीम्।
क्षुत्वतीं जृम्भमाणां वा न चासीनां यथासुखम्।।
नान्ज्यन्तीं स्वके नेत्रे व चाभ्यक्तामनावृताम्।
न पश्येत्प्रसवन्तीं च तेजस्कामो द्विजोत्तमः।।
न हीदृशमनायुष्यं लोके किन्जन विद्यते।

यादृशं पुरुषस्येह परदारोपसेवनम् ।।
यस्तु दोषवर्ती कन्यामनाख्यायोपपादयेत् ।
तस्य तद्वितथं कुर्यात्कन्यादातुर्दुरात्मनः ।।
विधिवत्प्रतिगृह्यापि त्यजेत्कन्यां विगर्हिताम् ।
व्याधितां विप्रदुष्टां वा छद्मना चोपपादिताम् ।।
तत्समुत्थो हि लोकस्य जायते वर्णसंडकरः ।
येन मूलहरोऽधर्मः सर्वनाशाय कल्पते ।।
स्त्रियं स्पृशेददेशे यः स्पृष्टो वा मर्षयेत्तथा ।
परस्परस्यानुमते सर्वं संग्रहणं स्मृतम् ।।
संवत्सरं प्रतीक्षेत द्विषन्तीं योषितं पतिः ।
ऊर्ध्वं संवत्सरात्त्वेनां दायं हृत्वा न संवसेत् ।
मद्यपाऽसाधुवृत्ता च प्रतिकूला च या भवेत् ।
व्याधिता वाऽधिवेत्तव्या हिंस्रार्थघ्नी च सर्वदा ।।
एतावानेव पुरुषो यज्जायाऽऽत्मा प्रजेति हि ।
विप्राः प्राहुस्तथा चैतद्यो भर्ता सा स्मृतांगना ।।
न निष्क्रयविसर्गाभ्यां भर्तुर्भार्या विमुच्यते ।
एवं धर्मं विजानीमः प्रजापतिनिर्मितम् ।।

If a man in this world is in control of his lust or subjugated by craving of sexual pleasure, whether he is a dumb or an intelligent one, can easily be deflected from his virtuous path by his wife or other ladies. A man should not sit even with his mother, sister or daughter on the same carpet because strong sexual senses can divert any erudite person from the moral path. The dynasty in which virtuous ladies suffer grief or be the cause of bereavement, is ruined, while if the morally high ladies do not experience any sorrow, become the cause of rise in that family's dignity and prolonged existence. It is the responsibility of husband or the head of family to take care of newly wedded wife, sick ladies and pregnant ladies and to offer them food without any delay before offering it to the guests and himself. A man who ever converse to achieve sexual amusement with a lady going through menstruation periods, diminishes his power, intelligence, age and discretion while the one who does not keep such sexual intentions, his aforesaid decorum are augmented. Man should not take meal in the same salver with any woman and he should not give a view to a lady who is sneezing, yawning, sitting with the intention of adultery in an isolated place, putting lampblack as a cosmetic in eyes, applying oil or lotion on body, almost naked or feeding a child. The prime reason which diminishes the spiritual power and age of the man is to sexually intercourse with strange lady or a lady other than wife. If during the time of *Panigrahan* or marriage ceremony, a bridegroom is cheated by giving a sinful girl or the one who possesses immoral persona then he can deny for the relationship. Man can divorce his wife who is defamed because of involving in illicit sexual relations, who suffers from incurable disease from the unmarried life and was not earlier informed to her husband or is involved in immoral activities or the one who is married by hiding her awful traits thereby betraying to her husband. If a man intercourses with a lady other than his wife then this becomes the prime cause of cross-breed generation and such immoral act itself becomes the origin of unpardonable transgression which ultimately

106

ruins the outcome of all the religious acts performed in the whole of life span. A man should not touch other lady with sexual intentions and should not give the silence acquiescence if she does the same. A man of virtuous conduct should give one year's duration to his relationship with wife who keeps animosity for him so that she may improve herself and become of proper behavior. If still there is no improvement in her disposition then he should give away all the items she has brought and take what ever he has given to her after marriage and should not intercourse with her. A husband may divorce his wife if she intakes alcoholic beverages, keeps illicit sexual relations with others, always shows improper behavior or performs against the righteous act done by him, is suffering from incurable disease or is sexually impotent, is of violent nature and spends lot of money in immoral or anti social activities. After this, when a husband decides to isolate his wife, he is warned by religious saying that a man is complete by his own body, wife and children. Thus the entity of a husband is not different form his wife. Husband and wife cannot be separated by the mere physical isolation or by the process of divorce. If a man divorces his sexually corrupt and ill natured wife or relinquishes the moral control over her, then also a wife can not get emancipated from her duties towards the family because the husband-wife relationship is destined by Lord *Brahama*. The directions are given in *Brahadaranyak Upnishad* that how a man should behave with his wife who possesses immoral attitude and denies performing sexual intercourse with husband without any proper reason.

सा चेदस्मै न दद्यात्कामेनामवक्रीणीयात् सा चेदस्मै नैव
दद्यात्काममेनां यष्ट्या वा पाणिना वोपहत्यातिक्रामेदिन्द्रियेण
ते यशसा यश आदद इत्ययश एव भवति ।।

If a lady is not devoting herself and shows reluctance in love making or sexual intercourse without any proper cause then the man should not coerce her instead he should try to gratify her requirements. After this also, if there is no change in her attitude, then he should try to frighten her by the threat of punishments. In such intimidations of punishments, man should warn his wife that he too shall pay no attention to her and reduce his feelings for her. If man starts avoiding his wife and does not express his sexual desire for her, she will initiate by devoting herself for sexual mating. In *Vishnu Puran*, the directions are given to men concerning sexual relations as follows:-

नान्ययोनावयोनौ वा नोपयक्तौषधस्तथा ।
द्विजदेवगुरूणां च व्यवायी नाश्रमे भवेत् ।।
चैत्यचत्वरतीर्थेषु नैव गोष्ठे चतुष्पथे ।
नैव श्मशानोपवने सलिलेषु महीपते ।।
प्रोक्तपर्वस्वशेषेषु नैव भूपाल सन्ध्ययो: ।

गच्छेद्व्यवायं मतिमात्र मूत्रोन्चारपीडितः ।।
पर्वस्वभिगमोऽधन्यो दिवा पापप्रदो नृप ।
भुवि रोगावहो नृणाम्प्रशस्तो जलाशये ।।
परदारान्न गच्छेन्च मनसापि कथन्चन ।
किमु वाचास्थिबन्धोऽपि नास्ति तेषु व्यवायिनाम् ।।
ऋतावुपगमश्शस्तस्स्वपत्ल्यामवनीपते ।
पुत्रामक्षे शुभे काले ज्येष्ठायुग्मासु रात्रिषु ।।
नाधूनां तु स्त्रियं गच्छेन्नातुरां न राजस्वलाम् ।
नानिष्टां न प्रकुपितां न त्रस्तां न च गर्भिणीम् ।।
नादक्षिणां नान्यकामां नाकामां नान्ययोषितम् ।
क्षुत्क्षामां नातिभुक्तां वा स्वयं चैभिर्गुणैर्युतः ।।
मृतो नरकमभ्येति हीयतेऽत्रापि चायुषः ।
परदाररतिः पुंसामिह चामुत्र भीतिदा ।।

To perform sexual intercourse with cow or any other animal, with some other artificial object, during the addiction of some intoxicated medicine or alcoholic beverage and within the premises of the sanctuary of the Guru, is forbidden. Man is not permitted to perform sexual play under the shelter of spring tree, at the patio, at a pilgrimage place, at cattle house, at crossroads or publicly, at a place near funeral ground or graveyard, in a park or garden and in water. A man should not even think of committing sexual coalition with a lady other than his wife, touching the other lady or talking to her in context of sexual pleasure is far away. The reason behind is that the sexual mating done by physically, verbally or even in thoughts with other woman vanishes the captivity of bones in the next incarnations thereby the next birth which such person shall take will be of insect. During the time of *Ritukal* or the unsafe period after menstruation, husband is allowed to have sex with his wife. It is good to sexually intercourse with the wife during the early pious moment of the three hours of the night of a paired masculine lunar asterism. If wife is despondent, ailing, *Rajaswala* or menstruating, reluctant or is not feeling like to have intercourse thereby lying on the bed like a corpse and starving or overindulged, then a man should not perform mating with her. He should not carry out sexual intercourse even if he is having the same aforementioned situations or symptoms with him. The sensual allure or infatuations for a lady other than own wife becomes the cause of anguish and sorrow in this world as well as in the next world after death. In this life, his age reduces and the worth of the moral attributes done by him in past diminishes while after death he occupies hell. In *Devi Bhagwat Mahapuran*, a man is directed in context of ladies in following ways:-

स्त्रीपुंवन्च गृहे येषां गृहिणां स्त्रीवशः पुमान् ।।
निष्फलञ्च जन्म तेषामशुभञ्च पदे पदे।
मुखे दुष्टा योनिदुष्टा यस्य स्त्री कलहप्रिया ।।
अरण्यं तेन गन्तव्यं महारण्यं गृहाद्वरम्।
सततं सुलभा तत्र न तेषां गृह एव च।
वरमग्नौ स्थितिर्हिन्नजन्तूनां सन्निधौ सुखम् ।।
ततोऽपि दुःखं पुंसाञ्च दुष्टस्त्रीसन्निधौ ध्रुवम्।
व्याधिज्वाला विषज्वाला वरं पुंसां वरानने ।।
दुष्टस्त्रीणां मुखज्वाला मरणादतिरिच्यते।
पुमाञ्च स्त्रीजिताञ्चैव भस्मान्तं शौचमध्रुवम् ।।

110

यदहि कुरुते कर्म न तस्य फलभाग्भवेत् ।
निन्दितोऽत्र परत्रैव सर्वत्र नरकं व्रजेत् ।।
जीवन्मृतोऽशुचिर्दुःखी दुःशीलापतिरेव च ।।
निर्दोषकामिनीत्यागं करोति यो नवे भुवि ।
स याति नरकं घोरं किन्तु सर्वेश्वरोऽपि वा ।।

The house, in which wife behaves like a man or possesses mannish attitudes and husband acts just like a subservient of her or is obligated to pursue her, life of husband becomes worthless and disgraceful. A man, whose wife is of very cruel nature, carries extreme shrewd feelings, possesses adulterated character because of involvement in sexual debauchment and is of hostile temperament, should spend his rest of the life tranquilly in a forest because his residence is just like a hell for him. A man is more troubled by the vindictive conduct and harsh vocalizations of his wife than by the suffering from an ailment, physical pain and craving for sexual delight. Such ladies become the cause of perpetual bereavement for their husbands. A man, who acts according to the instructions given by his wife without applying his own power of discretion and conscience and is presided over by his wife, himself diminishes the fortunate outcome of all the upright religious deeds done by him in the whole of his life span and is slandered in this world as well as in the next world after death. Ultimately such men occupy ever lasting hell after death. A man, who is husband to a lady involved in adultery, is like a cadaver even after being alive. In contrast of this, a

husband who physically or mentally harasses, chastises o
divorces his innocent and virtuous wife, always attains the
worst hell after death. In *Bhavishya Puran*, men are directed in
the following ways:-

गुरूपत्नीं तु युवतीं नाभिवादेत पादयोः ।
पूर्णविंशतिवर्षेण गुणदोषौ विजानता ।।
स्वभाव एवं नारीणां नराणामिह दूषणम् ।
अतोर्थात्र प्रमाद्यन्ति प्रतिपाद्य विपश्चितः ।।
अविद्वांसमलं लोके विद्वांसमपि व पुनः ।
प्रमदा ह्यत्पंथ नेतुं कामक्रोधवशानुगम् ।।
मात्रा स्वस्रा दुहित्रा वा न विविक्तासनो भवेत् ।
बलवानिन्द्रियग्रामो विद्वांसमपि कर्षति ।।
अनुरूपे कुले जातां श्रुतवित्तक्रियादिभिः ।
लभेतानिन्दितां कन्या मनोज्ञां धर्मसाधनाम् ।।
पुमानर्थमांस्तावद्यावद्धार्या न विदन्ति ।
तस्माद्यथाक्रमं काले कुर्याद्धारपरिग्रहम् ।।
असमैर्निन्द्यते सद्भिरुत्तमैः परिभूयते ।
तुल्यैः प्रशस्यते यस्मात्तस्मात्साधुतमो मतः ।।

- - - - - - -

आकांक्षेताष्टवर्षाणि भर्तापि प्रसवं स्त्रियाः ।।
स्त्रीणां धर्मार्थकामेषु नातिसन्धानमाचरेत् ।
तासां तेष्वभिसन्धानाद्विवेदात्माभिसंहितः ।।
जायात्वर्धं शरीरस्य नृणां धर्मादिसाधने ।
नातस्तासु व्यथा । काञ्चित्प्रतिकूलं समाचरेत् ।।

If the wife of Guru is young then a young disciple, who
keeps the conscience or the capability of discretion to
distinguish between decent and indecent behavior, should not
pay regards to her by touching her feet because in this world,

112

it is a frequent propensity of human beings to get enthralled towards peccadillo. A man of morals never gets unacquainted with the disposition of women hence always be attentive to keep himself away from the other women. Ladies can deflect even an erudite man from his virtuous path. A man should not sit even with his mother, sister and daughter in an isolated place because the group of senses causing sexual yearning is very influential. A person should marry with a girl of equivalent dynasty, having almost same mental level, of equivalent or lesser qualification and with the one who belongs to the same financial status. A man is not complete until he marries, so he should marry at the appropriate age. To marry with a girl who is not of equivalent financial and moral status is unfortunate. A man is defiled in his marital life if he marries in a family of comparatively superior financial status while gets morally degraded if marries a girl of low standard. Thus, a man should marry a girl of the family equivalent to his own financial and social standing. A man should wait for eight years for his wife to become pregnant and then he should take any decision after judging the infertility in himself or in his wife. If a man betrays his innocent, virtuous and faithful wife in the matters related to finance, religion and sexual relations, then he is actually cheating his own soul. According to Hindu mythology, a wife is the exact half part of her husband's entity therefore an ethically strong and praiseworthy wife should not be treated shoddily. According to *Bahvishya Puran*:-

न हीदृश्मनायुष्यं लोके किश्चन विद्यते।
यादृशं पुरुषस्येह परदारोपसेवनम्।
न चेर्ष्या स्त्रीषु कर्तव्या दारा रक्ष्याः प्रयत्नतः।
अनायुष्या भवेदीर्ष्या तस्माक्तां परिवर्जयेत्।
सुवासिनीं गुर्विणीं च वृद्धांबालातुरांस्तथा।
भोजयेत्संकृतात्रेन प्रथमं चरमं गृही ।।
च चास्नातां स्त्रियं गच्छेद्गर्भिणीं न रजस्वलाम्।
नानिष्टां वै न कुपितां नाशस्तां न च रोगिणीम् ।।
नादक्षिणां नान्यकामां नाकामां नान्ययोषितम्।
सुक्षामामत्यभुक्ता च स्वयं चैभिर्गुणैर्युतः ।।
गुरोः पतिव्रतानां च तथा यज्ञतपस्विनाम्।
परीवादं न कुर्वीत परिहासेऽपि भारत ।।

The main reason behind the deterioration in the age of
a man is his involvement in adultery. A man should not be
jealous of ladies instead he should give his full effort in
protecting them from their own lust. It is the responsibility of
men to feed first to newly wedded wife, pregnant ladies, old
ladies and to small children as a prime obligation. A man
should not sexually intercourse with a lady who is impure or
physically unclean, pregnant, *Rajaswala* or menstruating,
having harmful intentions, angry natured, physically unwell,
dumb, mentally sick or having any sort of mental disorder, not
willing or keeps love for other man, lacking sexual feeling,
another's women, starving and overindulged. One should not
speak against of Gurus, husband devotee wives and saints
even in amusements or in bantering. In *Srimadbhagwat*

*Mahapuran*, men are directed in context of ladies in the following way:-

जह्याद् यदर्थे स्वप्राणान्हन्याद् वा पितरं गुरूम् ।
तस्यां स्वतं स्त्रियां जह्याद् यस्तेन ह्याजितोजितः ।।
यदि न स्याद् गृहे माता पत्नी वा पतिदेवता ।
व्यंगे रथ इव प्राज्ञः को नामासीत दीनवत् ।।

Men are found to commit suicide in the pseudo affection or infatuation with ladies. They often rupture the relationship with their parents and brothers on the directions of wife. A man who diverts himself from the infatuation with such ladies or with own wife, occupies space in the feet of God. A house without the presence of mother or a husband devotee wife is just like a chariot without wheels thus a wise man cannot live over there. Lord *Krishan* says in *Bhagwat Gita* that:-

यततो ह्यपि कौन्तेय पुरुषस्य विपश्चितः ।
इन्द्रियाणि प्रमाथीनि हरन्ति प्रसभं मनः ।।

Senses are so powerful that they can deflect even an intellectual and sensible man from his moral path. Thus, a person should have a proper control over his senses. It is revealed in *Markandeya Mahapuran* that:-

रक्षेद्दारान्त्यजेदीर्षा दिवा च स्वप्नमैथुने ।
नग्रां परस्त्रियं नेक्षेत्र पश्येदात्मनः शकृत् ।
उदक्यादर्शनं स्पर्शो वर्ज्यं सम्भाषणं तथा ।

A man should not even think about performing sexual intercourse or sleeping during the day time and should not even think of contemplating to other lady who is unclothed. Men should not deliberately look, touch or converse to a *Ritumati* or menstruating lady. In *Mahabharat*, men have been directed extensively in context of ladies in the following way:-

तृष्णाभिभूतस्तैर्बद्धस्तानेवाभिपरिप्लवन् ।
ससारतन्त्रवाहिन्यस्तत्र बुद्धयेत योषितः ।।
प्रकृत्या क्षेत्रभूतास्ता नराः क्षेत्रज्ञलक्षणाः ।
तस्मादेवाविशेषेण नरोऽतीयाद् विशेषतः ।।
कृत्या होता घोररूपा मोहयन्त्यविचक्षणान् ।
रजस्यन्तर्हिता मूर्तिरिन्द्रियाणां सजातनी ।।
नेक्षेतादित्यमुद्यन्तं न नग्नां परस्त्रियम ।
मैथुन । सततं धर्म्ये गुह्ये चैव समाचरेत् ।।

— — — — — — — — — — — — — — — —

सह स्त्रियाथ शयनं सह भोज्यं च वर्जयेत् ।।

A man who is overwhelmed with the yearning of sexual pleasure and pseudo self-esteem, for him a lady is like trap of illusion and infatuation. Ladies are equivalent to the nature hence they have a beautiful looking visible existence while men walk on this nature hence they are the spectators. Women attract men by their mortal exquisiteness in the same way as people are attracted towards the gorgeousness of nature. Thus men should not take special efforts to achieve the propinquity of such wonderful looking mysterious ladies. These ladies are just like *Kritya*, a dreadful female deity to

116

whom sacrifices are offered for magical purpose, who trap the men in the snares of their deceptive globe. Ladies, who possess *Rajogun* or alluring qualities, create the disorder of the senses. Men should not stare at rising sun and a stripped lady. During the period of *Ritukal* or the unsafe period, man should sexually intercourse with his wife in an isolated place as per the religious saying. After sexual union, man and woman should not slumber at the same bed and nor should eat from the same salver. According to *Agni Puran*:-

स्त्रीणामीर्षा न कर्तव्या विश्वासं तासु वर्जयेत् ।।

A man should neither be jealous of woman and nor should trust them. According to *Sanyasoapanishad*, an aged lady is also neither detached nor trustworthy in context of sexual relations.

सुजीर्णोऽपि सुजीर्णासु विद्वांस्त्रीषु न विश्वसेत् ।
सुजीर्णास्वपि कन्थासु सजते जीर्णमम्बरम् ।।

A wise man after attaining the old age should not trust even on an old lady in context of sexual desire because an obsolete item of clothing is needed to be darned by the piece of some other old torn cloth. According to *Mahabharat*:-

त्दा चैतत् कुलं नास्ति यदा शोचन्ति जामयः ।।
जामीशप्तानि गेहानि निकृत्तानीव कृत्यया ।
स्त्रियो यत्र च पूज्यन्ते रमन्ते तत्र देवताः ।।
अपूजिताश्रच यत्रैता: सर्वास्तत्राफला: क्रिया: ।

The family where morally high daughters or virtuous daughter-in-laws undergo bereavement, the impression and future of that dynasty is ruined by the curse of those praiseworthy ladies because a distressing lady cannot see the contentment of others. If any house is cursed by these ladies while lamenting piercingly then that house is devastated by the atrocious female deities. The place where noble and strong character ladies are appreciated and respected Goddess make that house their own residence while the place where such respected and worthy women are affronted, there the outcome of all ritual processes go into vain. In the *Manu Smriti*, the aforesaid mentioned description is expressed in the following way:-

यत्र नार्यस्तु पूज्यन्ते रमन्ते तत्र देवताः।
यत्रेतास्तु न पूज्यन्ते सर्वास्तत्राफलाः क्रियाः।

According to *Shastras*, a girl who possesses decent personality and knowledge is said to be the best. Such girls may belong to any dynasty, their community or category becomes ineffectual in front of their virtuous qualities.

स्त्रीरत्नं दुष्कुलान्चापि विषादप्यमृतं पिवेत्।
अदूष्या हि स्त्रियो रत्नमाप इत्येव धर्मतः॥

If a girl belonging to a lower community or a financially poor family possesses upright qualities, then she could be accepted for marriage in the same way as nectar of the God or ambrosia is taken immediately even if it comes out from the source of poison or a poisonous place. This is because high moral ladies, authentic jewels and pure water are not polluted by their source of origin. According to *Matsya Puran*, men have been directed the following:-

न माता न पिता न स्त्री न ऋत्विग्याज्यमानवा: अन्योन्यं पतितास्त्याज्या योगे दण्डया: ।

Parents, wife, family priest or provider of traditional ritualistic service and the one who requests and pays for performance of a sacrifice or traditional service can not be abandoned even if they are mistaken. According to *Brahama Puran*, the commendable deeds that should be done by the men are expressed as the following:-

नरकस्येव मूर्खाणां कामोपहतचेतसाम् ।

पुत्रेषु चैव पौत्रेषु को न कुर्यात्सुखं रवे ।
करोति य: कन्यकानां स संपद्भाजनं भवेत् ।।
नग्नां परस्त्रियं नेक्षेत्र पश्येदात्मन: शकृत् ।
उदक्यादर्शनस्पर्शमेवं संभाषणं तथा ।।

परदारा न गन्तव्या: पुरूषेण विपश्चिता ।।
इष्टापूर्तायुषां हन्त्री परदारगतिर्नृणाम् ।
न हीदृशमनायुष्यं लोके किंचन विद्यते ।
रक्षेद्दारांस्त्यजेदीर्ष्या तथाऽहि स्वप्नमैथुने ।

नाऽऽऽलपेज्जनविद्विष्टान्वीरहीनास्तथा स्त्रिय: ।

A young lady is like the entrance to hell for those imprudent men who are always involved in sexual activities.

119

All human beings take effort to give birth to a son but the person who keeps the desire of a daughter is the best among others. Man should not see a nude lady and his own excrement. It is strictly prohibited for men to deliberately have a look, converse and touch a lady who is *Rajaswala* or menstruating. A man should not intercourse with a lady other than his wife because such adultery shortens his lifespan and diminishes the outcome of the righteous deeds performed by him in the whole of lifespan. No deed is more disastrous and sinful than adultery. A man should not even think about sleeping and committing sexual mating in day time. Men should not keep any sort of conversation with the ladies who are sexually corrupt and the people involved in betraying the human race. In *Bhavishya Puran*, duties of the gents of the side of bride are mentioned in the following way:-

पूज्य एवं हि सम्बन्ध सर्वावस्थासु योषिताम् ।
कस्ततोऽप्युपकारांशं लिप्सेत कुलजः पुमान् ।।
सम्पूज्य स्वसुता तस्मै विधिवत्प्रतिपाद्यते ।
ततोऽस्या लिप्सते नाम किमकार्यमतः परम ।।
कन्यां प्रदाय यैवृत्तिरात्मनः परिकल्प्यते ।
दासभण्डनटादीनां मार्गोऽयं न महात्मनाम् ।।
तस्मात्स्त्रीबांधवा नित्यं प्रीतिमात्रैकसाधिनीम् ।
प्रतिपत्तिं समादध्युः सम्बन्धिभ्यः प्रसंगिनीम् ।

A lady at any stage of the age group or status is said to be reputable if she is of ethical conduct. A man of the family of such ladies should not keep the yearning for any kind of

120

financial profit or pecuniary advantage from them. After marrying the daughter, if parents keep the desire of financial profit from son-in-law then it is an unpardonable transgression. A person who possesses such craving is of very mean category and blemished character. After the marriage, bride's parents and pre-marriage relatives should keep limited relations with her.

# Instructions To Women

The directions to ladies and the duties of married ladies are described through the conversation between *Draupadi* and *Satyabhama* in *Mahabharata* as follows:-

नै यज्ञक्रियाः काश्चित्र श्राद्धं नोपवासकम् ।।

न तु भर्तरि शुश्रूषा तया स्वर्गे जयत्सुत ।
उद्विग्नस्य कुतः शान्तिरशान्तस्य कुतः सुखम् ।
न जातु वशगो भर्ता स्त्रियाः स्यान्मन्त्रकर्मणा ।।
अमित्रप्रहितांश्चापि गदान् परमदारुणान् ।
मूलप्रचारैर्हि विषं प्रयच्छन्ति जिघांसवः ।।
जलोदरसमायुक्ताः श्विव्रिणः पलितास्तथा ।
अपुमांसः कृताः स्त्रीभिर्जडान्धबधिरास्तथा ।।
दुर्व्याहृताच्छद्दृकमाना दुःस्थिताद् दुर्वेक्षितात् ।
दुरासिताद् दुर्व्रजितादिगिताध्यासितादपि ।।

प्रमृष्टभाण्डा मृष्टात्रा काले भोजनदायिनी ।
संयता गुप्तधान्या च सुसम्मृष्टनिवेशना ।।
अतिरस्कृतसम्भाषा दुःस्त्रियो नानुसेवती ।
अनुकूलवती नित्यं भवाम्यनलसा सदा ।।

सर्वथा भर्तुरहितं न ममेष्टं कथंचन ।
यदा प्रवसते भर्ता कुटुम्बार्थेन केनचित् ।।
सुमनोवर्णकापेता भवामि व्रतचारिणी ।

यश्च भर्ता न पिबति यश्च भर्ता न सेवते ।।
यश्च नाश्नचति मे भर्ता सर्वे तद् वर्जयाम्यहम् ।

122

There is no need for a lady to perform ritualistic sacrificial act, after death rituals and any kind of observance or fasting. The one, who is husband devotee, gets rid from all misfortune and such lady need not worry to worship deities. A Lady, who is aggressive and perplexed, can never get unperturbed and consequently never attains abiding spiritual pleasure. A lady, who attempts to dominate her husband by applying incantations or black magic, is never succeeded because in such situation, she herself is culpable. It is also found that few dim-witted and wicked ladies use the medicines provided by enemies to subjugate their husbands and ultimately cause life loss or other kind of disabilities in the husbands. Somewhere enemies with the purpose of killing a man, provide his wife some poisonous item and tell her that if she feeds her husband with that item, then he will always act like a slave of her. Many ladies have attempted this and their husbands become handicapped or died.

*Draupadi* again says, "I always make sure to make my voice humble and polite and never speak ill of others, do not stand any where without any proper cause like uncivilized people, never stare other men like an unabashed lady, stay far from depraved conduct, never show brazenness while walking or in normal gestures, comprehend the needs of husband by the indications shown by him, always eat and bath when my husband and his relatives or friends have done it and sleep when my husband is slept, always keep the utensils clean, prepare food in hygienic way and provide food to others at proper time. I always be stubborn in controlling over my senses or desires, save grains and money clandestinely for the famine period to help my husband, keep my residence clean, never disrespect others, stay away from cunning and quarrelsome nature ladies, never show laziness, always behave according to my husband, never even communicate with men of no morals, stay away from discontent and ill speaking of others, never chortle or suppurate unnecessary and deafeningly, always speak truth and never betray my husband. I never like to stay in a place alone without the presence of my husband. Whenever all of my husbands go out of town with some work, I do not decorate myself with flowers or body lotions and always obstinate myself to follow asceticism like priestess. The edible items which my husband does not eat, I also leave eating those products. Though all of my husbands are of very gentle and courteous behavior but still I always make myself afraid of them just like people are scared of a poisonous snake because without fear, a lady can never be stable in love with a single man. I slumber after my husband, eat after him, never work against his directions and always respect my mother–in–law. These are the only ways by which a lady can keep her husband under control and the ladies of nasty behavior, who take help of some other ways to subjugate over their husbands, I never get effected by that." It is said in *Shastras* that:-

तत्संनिधौ यत् कथयेत् पतिस्ते यद्यप्यगुह्यं परिरक्षितव्यम् ।
मदं प्रमादं पुरुषेषु हित्वा संयच्छ भावं प्रतिगृह्म मौनम् ।
महाकुलीनाभिरपापिकाभिः स्त्रीभिः सतीभिस्तव सख्यमस्तु ।
चण्डाश्च शौण्डाश्च महाशनाश्च चौराश्च दुष्टाश्चपलाश्च वर्ज्याः ।

A wife should not divulge the secrets of her husband to others. She should give away the jealousy, arrogance and sensual lust for others and should never reveal her internal feelings. A lady should carry the camaraderie with only those ladies who belong to a dynasty of high morals and stay away from illicit activities. A lady should not live with the ladies who are aggressive by nature, alcoholic, eats too much, of haughty nature, involved in burgling, of vindictive nature, of depraved character and of flickering nature.

# Physical Imperfection of Women Based on Thei Activities

The description of physical disabilities in lades due to the activities they perform in their life are described in *Hariwans* *Mahapuran*. It is said that the ladies, who commi transgressions in their life span, endure physical or menta disorder and are cursed by God.

योषितुष्पफलानां च बालानां घातिनी तथा।
फलानां कर्तनकरी मातापितृवियोगिनी ।।
स्राविणी परगर्भाणां ततु ततु प्रायोपयोषिणी।
ईदृग्विधा भविष्यन्ति पन्चादोषयुताः स्त्रियः ।।
अपुष्पा मृतवत्साश्च काकवन्धयास्तथैव च।
कन्याप्रजालं च तथा स्रावयुक्ताः स्वपातकैः ।।

A lady who do not properly utilizes the fruits anc flowers and unnecessary destroys or pick them from trees slays the infants mentally or physically, slash fruits gratuitously, does the severance of the relations of the husband or other young men from their parents and brothers and aborts her pregnancy or helps out other ladies in doing so, endure five kinds of disorders termed as *Apushpa Mratvatsa*, *Kaakbandhya*, *Kanyapraja* and *Sravyukta*.

*Apushpa* means a lady who can not have the menstruations. A lady whose infant dies is said to be *Mratvatsa*. In *Kaakbandhya*, a lady can not conceive second

time. A lady who gives birth only to daughters is *Kanyapraja*.
A lady who suffers form self abortion is said to be *Sravyukta*.

# Conversations Regarding Women in *Dharamshastra*

In *DharmaShastra*, the statements regarding women are mostly based on mutual conversations. Few of such conversations are mentioned here in the following way:-

According to *Devi Bhagwat Mahapuran*, when *Shukdev* was requested by his father *Mahamuni Vyas* for his marriage he replied the following:-

स्त्रियं कृत्वा महाभाग! भवामि तद्वशानुगः ।
सुखं किं परतन्त्रस्य स्त्रीजितस्य विशेषतः ।।
विरामूत्रसम्भवो देहो नारीणां तन्मयस्तथा ।
कः प्रीतिं तत्र विप्रेन्द्र! विबुधः कर्तुमिच्छति ।।
गृह्णति पुरुषं यस्मादृगृहं तेन प्रकीर्तितम् ।
क सुखं बन्धनागारे तेन भीतोऽस्म्यहं पितः ।।
जलौकैव सदा नारी रुधिरं पिबतीति वै ।
मूर्खस्तु न विजानाति मोहितो भावचेष्टितैः ।।
भोगैर्वायैं धनं पूर्णं मनः कुटिलभाषणौः ।
कान्ता हरति सर्वस्वं कः स्तेनस्तादृशोऽपरः ।।

I don't want to get entangled in the deceptive world of a lady by marrying her. If I will marry then I too shall be subjugated by the awful shortcomings of women. The outcome of the virtuous deeds performed during whole of the lifespan vanishes if one is overpowered by the sexual lust of women. The life becomes worthless if man starts depending upon a lady and leads his life according to the directions provided by her. The body of ladies is full of excrements as stool and urine. A man can never be happy if he is interested in the filthy anus hole from where stool comes out and vaginal route which possess urine particles. A married man gets trapped by the snares of the illusory world made by his wife and forgets his ritualistic obligations while living with his family in the house therefore a house is said to be *Graha* or destined confinement provided by the conjunction of planets while wife is termed as *Grahani* or who overshadows men living in the house by her own appalling lifestyle, like an eclipse which occurs thereby shallows the virtuous qualities of sun or moon by demon *Rahu*. Therefore no man can be happy with this confinement laid upon him. Ladies are just like leeches that cling to men and suck their blood but unfortunately men could not comprehend this fact because of the illusion and infatuation created by women. A lady, through the sexual intercourse, sucks the seminal fluid, blood and upright attributes of men. In this way an endearing wife purloins everything form her beloved husband. According to *Srimad Bhagwat Mahapuran* the great ascetic *Dattatrey* has stated the following:-

दृष्ट्वा स्त्रियं देवसायां तद्वावैरजितेन्द्रियः ।
प्रलोभितः पतत्यन्धे तमस्यग्नौ पतंगवत् ।।
पदापि युवतीं भिक्षुर्न स्पृशेद् दारवीमपि ।

स्पृशन् करीव बध्येत करिण्या अंगसंगतः ।।

- - - - - - - - - - - - - -

नाधिगच्छेत् स्त्रियं प्राज्ञः कर्हिचिन्मृत्युमात्मनः ।।

129

*Dattatrey* says, "I learned from a flying insect that as it goes near to the fire due to illusion and burns to die, similarly a man who is not having control over his senses, gets allured looking a woman body and gestures, hence looses his prudence and occupies the intense dark hell and destroys himself. I learned form male elephant that one should not touch even a portrait of a lady by mistake because the way, a male elephant becomes crazy to touch the wooden female elephant and falls in the trap made to seize him, similarly a man who touches the other lady falls in the chasm of moral decline. Any man who is full of discretion should not accept any lady in her body form for sexual pleasure because she is just like a living death of him." The conversation of fairy *Urvashi* and king *Pururva* is mentioned in *Devi Bhagwat Mahapuran*. *Urvashi* and *Pururva* were sexually spellbound to each other. When king beseech her for her love, she kept three condition in front of him of which if either is violated she shall leave king and go back to her own world. When the stipulation done by *Urvashi* with the king despoiled because of the illusion made by herself then she decided to go back to her world thereby leaving king alone. The king became very sentimental and started howling. She instructs the king in context of ladies as following:-

मूर्खोऽसि नृपशार्दूल ! ज्ञानं कुत्र गतं तव।

— — — — — — — — — — — — — — — — — —

कापि सख्यं न च स्त्रीणां वृकागमिव पार्थिव! ।।
न विश्वासो हि कर्तव्य: स्त्रीषु चौरेषु पार्थिवै: ।

Oh king! You are very imprudent. What happened with
your discretion power? All ladies are callous like a wolf and
possess depraved internal feelings. Ladies are emotionless
and merciless hence they do not love any one. In fact they
illustrate their fake emotions and pseudo affection to attain
sexual pleasure. Kings on the earth should not trust on ladies
and thieves. In *Bhagwat Gita*, during the conversation of
*Krishna* and *Arjun, Arjun* says the following:-

अधर्माभिभवात्कृष्ण प्रदुष्यन्ति कुलस्त्रिय:।
स्त्रीषु दुष्टासु वार्ष्णेय जायते वर्णसंङ्कर: ।।
संङ्करो नरकायैव कुलघ्नानां कुलस्य च।
पतन्ति पितरो ह्येषां लुप्तपिण्डोदकक्रिया: ।।
दोषैरेतै: कुलघ्नानां वर्णसंङ्करकारकै: ।
उत्साद्यन्ते जातिधर्मा: कुलधर्माश्च शाश्वता: ।।

When expansion of impiety occurs in a dynasty then
the ladies of that family get sexually polluted and commit
debauchery and hence give birth to crossbreed in the form of
unwanted illegitimate progenies. Due to the birth of unwanted
and immoral offspring, the head of the dynasty and dynasty it
self faces the hell like situation. The ancestors of such
dynasties get besmirched and religiously lapsed as they lack
praiseworthy successors for the after death rituals because of

unlawfully born and non worthy children in the forthcoming generations or cross-breed successors. Such descendants in the family destroy the honor of the dynasty and further produce immoral children. By giving birth to cross-breeds they deteriorate all of the auspicious outcomes of high leveled virtuous deeds performed by forefathers in the past.

Who seeks more pleasure among a man and a woman during sexual intercourse? In this context, *Yudhisthir* keeps his doubt in front of *Bheeshma*. Then *Bheeshma* elaborates the case of king *Bhangaswan*. King had several offspring but some how due to destiny, in future, he became female. Being a woman he accepted a man as his husband and gave birth to progenies. His all children were living in the palace very happily meantime lord *Indra* cursed him therefore his children fought amongst themselves and died. King requested *Indra* to forgive him then lord *Indra* asked the king, who was still a woman, to choose any one group of children to make alive out of two groups that he had being in male form and in female form.

तापसी तु ततः शक्रमुवाच प्रयतान्जलिः ।
स्त्री भूतान्य हि ये पुत्रास्ते मे जीवन्तु वासव ।।
स्त्रियास्त्वभ्यधिकः स्नेहो न तथा पुरूषस्य वै ।
तस्मात् ते शक्र जीवन्तु ये जाताः स्त्रीकृतस्य वै ।।
स्त्रीत्वमेव वृणे शक्र पुंस्तवं नेच्छामि वासव ।

132

एवमुक्तस्तु देवेन्द्रस्तां स्त्रियं प्रत्युवाच ह।
स्त्रियाः पुरुषसंयोगे प्रीतिरभ्यधिका सदा।
एतस्मात् कारणाच्छक्र स्त्रीत्वमेव वृणोम्यहम्।।

The king in the form of woman said that he wants the set of children to be alive which were born after he became woman because no child is more beloved to a lady than her own son and a mother has more affection towards the progenies than a father. Lord *Indra* asked king whether he wants to be in the form of a lady or in the earlier form of man. The king replied, "I want to be in the form of a woman because comparatively a woman seeks more pleasure during the time of sexual intercourse than a man."

The conversation of *Yam* and *Yami*, who were real brother and sister, is mentioned in *Shree Narsingh Puran*. *Yami*, who was unknown to process and the objectives of marriage, once visited the custom of a marriage ceremony hence being surprised put his queries to *Yam*, her brother, about this. *Yam* told her the intention and significance of marriage. *Yami* got infatuated by the delusion created by lord of love and sex, *Kamdeva*, hence beseeched *Yam* to marry with her and proposed him to be her companion in sexual mating.

कामार्तायाः स्त्रियाः कान्त वशगो भव मा चिरम्।
स्वेन कायेन मे कायं संयोजयितुमर्हसि।।
न ते संयोजयिष्यामि कायं कायेन भामिनि।

न भ्राता मदनार्ताया: स्वसु: कामं प्रयच्छति ।।
- - - - - - - - - - - - - - - - -
मुनय: पापमाहुस्तं य: स्वसारं निगृह्णति ।।

Yami says to her brother that she was having intense craving for sexual mating, so let the union of their bodies happen through mating and he should let his emotions and feelings to get subjugated by her sexual yearning. Yam replies to her, "I can not let the union of our bodies happen because no ethical man can even think about satisfying the sexual need of his own real sister. The one who does so or performs sexual relation with his sister, is of despicable mindset as it is one of the most deplorable and unpardonable transgression and such person occupies hell after death." Conversation of Devyani and Kach is stated in Matsya Puran. Kach was a young faithful devotee of the Shukracharya, the well known guru of monsters whereas Devyani was his daughter. Devyani requests and implore Kach for marriage but he does not give his consent on her request.

गृहाण पाणिं विधिवन्मम मन्त्रपुरस्कृतम् ।।
यथा मम गुरुर्नित्यं मान्य: शुक्र: पिता तव ।
देवयानि तथैव त्वं नैवं मां वक्तुमर्हसि ।
गुरूपुत्रीति कृत्वाऽहं प्रत्याख्यास्ये न दोषत: ।
गुरुणा चाभ्यनुज्ञात: काममेवं शपस्व माम् ।।

On the request of Devyani, Kach replies, "You are the daughter of my Guru hence are also equivalent respectable and praiseworthy to me as my guru is. For this only reason,

134

request you not to have sexual conversation with me as I can not marry you. You have no imperfection but I am constrained by my ethics and as per my own doctrine, one should not marry with his guru's daughter because any lady of guru's family is at the place of mother for a true disciple."

The ladies who are erudite and husband devotee also suffer from hallucination which make them of pessimistic assessment. Sometimes they even fallaciously accuse on a priest. During the period spent in exile, in a forest, *Sita* requested to her husband lord *Ram* to chase a beautiful deer for deer-skin thus *Ram* left behind his younger brother for the security of her and went to chase the deer. *Ram* ordered *Laxman* not to leave *Sita* alone until he return. Meantime *Rawan's* follower in the form of deer called on for *Laxman* in the voice of *Ram* so that *Laxman* might come to help *Ram* thereby leaving *Sita* alone. *Laxman* was familiar with the divine personality of *Ram* therefore he did not become influenced with that but *Sita* got depressed and asked *Laxman* to go to help *Ram*. *Laxman* tried to elucidate *Sita* that *Ram* was secure and he can not leave her unaccompanied. *Sita* even being a very husband devotee and knowledgeable lady, got influenced by the hallucination and blamed *Laxman* in an unabashed manner. This is stated in *Devi Bhagwat Mahapuran* as following:-

अहं जानामि सौमित्रे ! सानुरागं च मां प्रति।
प्रेरितं भरतेनैव मदर्थमिह सड्त्तम।।
नाहं तथाविधो नारी स्वैरिणी कुहकाधम।
मृते रामे पतिं त्वां न कर्तुमिच्छामि कामतः।।

This is also stated in *Narsingh Puran*:-

मृते रामे तु मामिच्छत्रतस्त्वं न गमिष्यसि।
इन्युक्त : स विनीतात्मा असत्रप्रियं वचः।।

"I have understood that you are infatuated with me and want to physically accept me as a wife. You are performing such offense under the deceitful guidance of your other brother *Bharat*. You want your brother lord *Ram* to die. I am a husband devotee and unsullied lady hence you can never physically get me even in the absence of my husband."

In *Shastras* there are many examples which have proved that ladies are the only reason causing annoyance and sexual perversion in men. A lady never advices her husband to be calm and merciful instead provokes him by the word like coward, eunuch etc. In *Mahabharat*, *Draupadi* says to her husband *Yudhisthir* the following:-

नूनं च तव वै नास्ति मन्युर्भरतसत्तम।
यत् ते भ्रातृश्च मां चैव दृष्ट्वा न व्यथते मनः।।

"It is true that your heart is lacking of obligatory aggression and self-esteem and you have become coward because you don't feel any grief finding me and your other brothers distressed." Here *Draupadi* mentioned her own

136

troubles as well as the problem of *Yudhisthir*'s brothers because those all were her husband. In case if they would not have been her husbands then she would have never included their grief over here. It is mentioned in *Narsingh Puran* that demoness *Surpankha*, in the deceptive appearance of a beautiful lady, approaches to *Ram* and says:-

अतीव निपुणा चाहं रतिकर्मणि राघव ।
त्यक्त्वैनामनभिज्ञां त्वं सीतां मां भज शोभनाम् ।।
इत्याकर्ण्य वचः प्राह रामस्तां धर्मतत्परः ।
परस्त्रियं न गच्छेऽहं गच्छ लक्ष्मणम् ।।

"Oh *Ram*! I am expertise in sexual art and *Sita* stands nowhere in front of my sexual skills thus you leave her and accept me." *Ram* replies to her, "I do not keep relations with other ladies. *Laxman* is unmarried, so you go and request to him." Finding such aversion and evasion in Lord *Ram* for her, she requests him to write a letter on the name of *Laxman* otherwise he too shall refuse. *Ram* being the omniscient was able to recognize fiendish *Surpankha* in the form of a beautiful lady. *Ram* wrote a latter to *Laxman* instructing to cut the nose and ear of the person coming with that message. *Laxman* was unmarried and he would not be able to recognize the *Surpankha*'s actual appearance behind her pseudo beautiful looking form. When *Laxman* read that, he cut the nose and ear of the gorgeous appearing lady and then she altered into her original disgusting form of demoness and left from there weeping. Depraved, fraudulent and wicked natured ladies

137

desire for what kind of behavior form there husbands, is mentioned in *Hariwansh Puran*:-

तस्य भार्यातिदुष्टा च कर्कशा कलहप्रिया।
असत्यालापनिपुणा परद्वेषपरायणा।।
हृत्वा चक्रे धनस्यापि संग्रहं पापनिश्चया।

- - - - - - - - - -

एकान्ते भक्षणं चक्रे भर्तर्यत्रं प्रशुष्ककम्।।
दुराग्रहा दुष्टमनाः पतिनिन्दापरायणा।
बहुपापप्रकर्त्री च परवेश्मोपवेशिनी।।
सौभाग्यास्ताः स्त्रियो लोके यासामुद्योगशालिनः।
पतयो धनधान्यादिसमृद्धिपरिशोभिताः।।
ते वै स्त्रीणां वाक्यकराः शिशुपालनतत्पराः।
नित्यं गृहेषु तिष्ठन्ति स्त्रीणां संतोषकारकाः।।
सदन्नभक्षणात् पुष्टा भार्याज्ञापरिपालकाः।
व्यवसायं च भार्याणां कुर्वन्ति बुद्धिशालिनः।

"His wife was of utter shrewd nature and harsh speaking. She loved unnecessary quarreling, attempted pilfering with harmful intentions and was expertise in lying. She used to eat rich food alone while giving remnants of it to her husband. She was very stubborn with malevolent intent and used to speak ill of her husband in his absence. She used to say that only those ladies are fortunate whose husbands are wealthy, take the charge of children, every time stand like a slave in front of wives, satisfy their wives completely, fulfil all desires of the wives, obedient to wives hence never apply own discretion power and are wise but perform or act as directed by the wives." In context of ladies, the colloquy

138

between the sage *Ashtavakra* and an old lady *Disha* depicted in *Mahabharat* is of great importance. Old lady invites *Ashtavakra* for sexual intercourse but when he refuses her request, she says:-

नानिलोऽग्निर्न वरूणो न चान्ये त्रियशा द्विज।।
प्रिया: स्त्रीणां यथा कामो रतिशीला हि योषित:।
सहस्रे किल नारीणां प्राप्येतैका कदाचन।।
तथा शतसहस्रेषु यदि काचित् पतिव्रता।
नैता जानन्ति पितरं न कुलं न च मातरम्।।
न भ्रातृन् न च भर्तारं न च पुत्रान् न देवरान्।

— — — — — — — — — — — — —

लीलायन्त्य: कुलं घ्नन्ति कूलानीव सरिद्धरा:।
दोषान् सर्वोश्च मत्वाऽऽशु प्रजापतिरभाषत।।

— — — — — — — — — — —

अथ सा वेपमानांगी निमित्तं शीतजं तदा।।
व्यपदिश्य महर्षेर्वै शयनं व्यवरोहत।
स्वागतेनागतां तां तु भगवानभ्यभाषत।।
सोऽगृह्णद् भुजाभ्यां तु ऋषिं प्रीत्या नरर्षभम्।
निर्विकारमृषिं चापि काष्ठकुड्योपमं तदा।।
दु:खिता प्रेक्ष्य संजल्पमकार्षीद्रुषिणा सह।
ब्रह्मत्कामतोऽन्यास्ति स्त्रीणां पुरुषतो धृति:।।
कामेन मोहिता चाहं त्वां भजन्तीं भजस्व माम्।
प्रहृष्टो भव विप्रर्षे समागच्छ मया सह।।
सर्वान् कामानुपाश्नीमो ये दिव्या ये च मानुषा:।
नात: परं हि नारीणां विद्यते च कदाचन।।
यथा पुरुषसंसर्ग: परमेतद्विन: फलम्।

आत्मच्छन्देन वर्तन्ते नार्यो मन्मथचोदिताः ।।
न च दह्यन्ति गच्छन्तयः सुतप्तैरपि पांसुभिः ।
परदारानहं भद्रे न गच्छेयं कथंचन ।।
दूषितं धर्मशास्त्रज्ञैः परदाराभिमर्शनम् ।
स्थविराणामपि स्त्रीणां बाधते मैथुनज्वरः ।।

"A lady does not keep such devotion even to eternal, veritable and discernible Gods like *Agni Dev,* the god of fire and *Varun Dev,* the lord of sky as she possesses for the man with whom she attains sexual satisfaction. Ladies are always desirous for luxurious life and sexual pleasure, by nature. Seldom there would be any lady in thousands whose mind is not allured towards sexual pleasure and hardly ever a lady in millions is found to be perfect devotee of her husband. Such fraudulent ladies pay no attention to the social standing of their parents as well as dignity of the dynasty and live a life of debauchery thereby vanishing the pride of their family in the same way as an ocean crosses its limit and obliterates the boundary at the shore." The old lady lay on the bed of sage by pretending herself getting frosty because of the freezing climate and embraced him to motivate sexually. She tried to sexually molest him but he remained snoozed on the bed, expressing no positive indications or movement, like a cadaver. Finding the sage to be entirely motionless and impervious, she says to him, "When a man is in the close proximity to a lady, she can not visualize anything except sexual contentment. I request you to have sexual coalition with me because nothing is more delightful and alluring for ladies than sexual pleasure. Ladies, with enduring ardent crave for sexual delight, are always ready for adultery and acts as per their own desire. A lady, impatient for sexual craving, if walks barefoot on the burning sand, does not suffer smarting. Sexual desire also troubles aged ladies." *Ashtavakra* says, "I cannot sexually intercourse with other lady because adultery is said to be an unpardonable transgression in the *Shastras*."

The conversation of *Twashti*, the wife of lord *Sun* and her father *Vishwakarma*, is depicted in *Matsya Puran* which deserves to be mentioned here. *Twashti* comes to her father's residence alone without informing to her husband. At this situation, *Vishwakarma* says to his daughter:-

यस्मादविज्ञाततया मत्सकाशमिहाऽऽगत ।
तस्मान्मदीयं भवनं प्रवेष्टुं न त्वमर्हसि ।।

"As you have come alone and without the consent of your husband, I shall not give my acquiescence to you to enter my residence." In *Matsya Puran*, through the conversation of *Shamishta* and *Yayati*, the situations are mentioned when one can verbalize fibs:-

न नर्मयुक्तं वचनं हिनस्ति न स्त्रीषु राजन्न विवाहकाले ।
प्राणात्यये सर्वधनापहारे पञ्चानृतान्याहुरपातकानि ।।

A fictitious converse in not sinful while bantering, during the discussion done in context of ladies, while talking to

women, in gossips done among women, in favor of a bride a
the occasion of her marriage, to save the own life or the life o
some other person and when every thing is lost in the life.

In the combat of *Mahabharat*, *Karna* was assassinated
by *Arjun* and finally war ends with the victory of *Pandavas*
*Kunti*, the mother of *Pandavas* divulge them that *Karna* was
also her son hence was the brother of them. *Yudhisthi*
whimpers that his brother *Karna* was put to death by another
brother *Arjun* and curse to women as following:-

पापेनासौ मथा श्रेष्ठो भ्राता ज्ञातिर्निपातितः ।
अतो मनसि यद् गुह्यं स्त्रीणां तत्र भविष्यति ।।

"I am the biggest sinner as I made one of my brother
killed by another younger brother because my mother did not
inform me about the veracity of the relations. I curse all the
women that from this instant no woman shall be capable to
keep any secret concealed".

# Rules of Purity and Impurity

In *Agni Puran*, the rules in context of purity-impurity of women are described as the following:-

नारीणां चैव वत्सानां शुकनीनां शुनो मुखम् ।

– – – – – – – ॐ – – – – – ॐ

मार्जारश्चडक्कमाच्छुद्धश्चतुर्थेऽहि रजस्वला ॥
स्नाता स्त्री पन्चमे योग्या देवे पित्र्ये च कर्मणि ।

– – – – – – – ॐ – – – – – ॐ

विवहितासु नाऽऽशौचं पितृपक्षे विधीयते ।
पितृगृहे प्रसूतानां विशुद्धिर्नैशिकी स्मृता ॥
सूतिका दशरात्रेण शुद्धिमाप्नोति नान्यथा ।
विवाहिता हि चेत्कन्या म्रियते पितृवेश्मनि ॥
स्त्रीणामकृतचूडाना विशुद्धिर्नैशिकी स्मृता ।
तथा च कृतचूडानां त्र्यहाच्छुध्यन्ति बान्धवाः ॥
त्रिभिर्मासतुल्याभिर्गर्भस्रावे त्र्यहेण वा ।
चातुर्मासिकपातान्ते दशाहं पन्चपासतः ॥
न स्नानं हि सपिण्डे स्यातिरात्रं सप्तमाष्टयोः ।
सद्यः शौचं सपिण्डानामा दन्तजननात्तथा ॥
अहस्त्वदत्तकन्यासु प्रदत्तासु त्र्यहं भवेत् ।
पक्षिणी संस्कृतास्वेव स्वस्रादिषु विधीयते ॥
पितृगोत्रं कुमारीणां व्यूढानां भर्तृगोत्रता ।
जलप्रदानं पित्रे च उद्वाहे चोभयत्र तु ॥
परपूर्वासु च स्त्रीषु त्रिरात्राच्छुद्धिरिष्यते ।
वृथा संकरजातानां प्रब्रज्यासु च तिष्ठताम् ॥
आत्मघाती चैकलक्षं वसेत्स नरकेऽशुचौ ।

143

अनौरसेषु पुत्रेषु भार्यास्वन्यगतासु च ।।
पाषण्डाश्रिता भर्तृघ्न्यो नाशौचोदकगाः स्त्रियः ।।

पुत्रो वा पुत्रिकाऽन्यो वा पिण्डं दद्याच्च पुत्रवत् ।।

The mouth of a praiseworthy and morally high woman is always unadulterated, a *Rajaswala* or menstruating lady becomes pure on fourth day, *Ritumati* lady or the lady with unsafe period after menstruations gets pure on fifth day and then becomes worthy to participate in after death rituals. A father is not adulterated on the death of married daughter. If a married lady gives birth to a child in father's home then impurity of one night is observed. The purity from *Sutika* or *Sutak* or the impurity because of the death of a person, who is directly related to the past seven generations from the father side, is obtained in ten days. If a married girl dies at father's place, then her father and brothers obtain purity after three nights. If a girl child dies before having the ritualistic process of *Mundan* or shaving the head or making bald, then impurity is imposed for one night but in case a girl dies after *Mundan* then impurity for the blood relatives is of three days.

A mother undergoes the impurity of three days or for the number of nights equal to the months of embryo on having miscarriage or self-abortion. This concept is applied for the miscarriage up to the forth and fifth months of pregnancy that impurity will be for the nights equal to the months of self aborted embryo. Due to miscarriage up to the sixth month

144

men of the *Sapind* are not adulterated hence are not obligated to take bath even. If self-abortion takes place in seventh and eight month then men of *Sapinda* carry three days impurity. A child, whose number of tooth is equal to his age in months, dies then there is no need for attaining purity for men of the family because in such case no adulteration is imposed upon the men.

Parents bear the impurity of one day if their daughter dies whose betrothal is yet not done and if she dies after her betrothal but before marriage then they seek the impurity of three days. If married sister or daughter dies, then the impurity imposed is of one day and one night. *Gotra* of an unmarried girl is same as of her father whereas married ladies have *Gotra* of their husband. On the demise of a married lady, both of her father and husband should pay holy water to her for the welfare of her soul in the next world.

A lady who lives with her second husband after divorcing the first one or the one who lives with other man without divorcing the husband, if dies then her husband or sons or other blood relatives purifies in three nights. One should not pay any kind of ritualistic homage to a crossbreed progeny or illegitimate offspring and to a person who suicides. No one should pay holy water in the bereavement of such person because a crossbreed son indicates adultery committed by forefathers and a person who commits suicide,

145

acquires hell for one million years. No one get impure on the demise of a lady committing harlotry, involved in hypocrisy and physically harassing her husband hence there is no need to pay holy water or any type of homage to her. Any person from the blood relatives, who is paying holy water or ritualistic homage to a dead, should perform such kind of after death rituals considering himself to be the son of dead one, as these rituals are done to set demised soul free of sensual temptations of the world.

# Widow Women

Hindu religion mentions transparent and stern rules for the married ladies who have become widow. Such regulations are not stated at the time of marriage because no body thinks of being a widow after marriage. According to *Manu Smriti:-*

नोद्वाहिकेषु मन्त्रेषु नियोगः कीर्तते क्वचित् ।
न विवाहविधावुक्तं विधवावेदनं पुनः ॥

In the specific sacred verses sanctified by *Vedas*, as spiritual instructions for performing marriage ceremony, there is no description available regarding *Niyog* process and widow-remarriage. If the betrothal is done while the marriage is still awaited and mean time would be bridegroom dies then that girl should be married to younger brother of demised bridegroom. If younger brother is not there or is not worthy of marriage then she can marry with some other man of her religion. According to *Manu Smriti-*:

यस्या म्रियेत कन्याया वाचा सत्ये कृते पतिः ।
तामनेन विधानेन निजो विन्देत देवरः ॥

If the would be bridegroom dies after the betrothal then his younger brother is the worthy bridegroom for that lady. If a bridegroom dies after marriage but before sexual intercourse with his wife then such lady is said to be virgin widow. If a man isolates with his wife due to her depraved behavior and illicit character but in future accepts her, on her apologizing, is also

147

considered to be remarriage and such lady is said to be Punarbhu. In fact the actual and broad meaning of Punarbhu is a woman who keeps sexual relations with other men along with her husband.

सा चेदक्षतयोनिः स्याद् गतप्रत्यागताऽपि वा।
पौनर्भवेन भर्त्रा सा पुनः संस्कारमर्हति।।

The marriage of a virgin widow, normal widow and remarriage of a divorced illicit character lady with the ex husband is legal and morally accepted. There are no restrictions on such marriages of widow ladies but it is said that if a widow marries then her second husband would not have right on her first husband's property.

अद्रव्यां मृतपत्नीं तु संगृह्त्रापराध्नुते।।

To marry a widow is not a sin instead very few courageous men dare to perform this righteous act. New husband shall not have any right on the demised previous husband's belongings. To keep sexual relations with widow without marrying her is strictly prohibited because she is considered to be a destitute. Hindu religion instructs the easy to-follow rules and regulations for women while stern rules for men. There are different provisions for widow and widower because a cross breed or illegitimate progeny is strictly opposed in religion. According to Manu Smriti-:

भार्यायै पूर्वमारिण्यै दत्वाग्नीनन्त्यकर्मणि पुनर्दारक्रियां
कुर्यात्तुनराधानमेव च।।

A widower can remarry to a widow, after performing the post death rituals including crimination of his deceased wife, in order to protect that widow or to give care to her children or to give birth to progenies. Such after death rituals is to be carried on for one year hence one can remarry at least after one year of the death of the spouse. It is believed that to carry the custom of generation, one male child is essential. Few intellectual religious saints believed to have two male kids essential. Though the after death obligations for a couple, not having any son, can be paid by other family members but such after death rituals performed are not considered to be done accurately. Any child brought to world through illicit sexual relations is considered to be illegitimate and this is also a reason that widows should marry so that they may not commit debauchment. According to *Manu Smriti*:-

नान्योत्पत्रा प्रजास्तीह न चाप्यन्यपरिग्रहे ।
न द्वितीयश्च साध्वीनां क्वचिद्द्वितोपदिश्यते ।।

A child, born because of sexual coalition with other man or other lady, is immoral and is not allowed to perform any religious service. A lady who is said to be husband devotee never thinks of another man if her husband is alive.

A lady, who becomes widow, should keep herself busy with her children in performing the responsibilities. A widow is free to marry any man having equivalent circumstances as of her own. Again if she does not possess any children then she

149

is strictly instructed to remarry but if she does not want to remarry and has no child then she has to adopt a child so that she may be busy in a noble cause because a widow who does not marry and possess no child, is always found to be involved in illicit sexual relations. If husband is having some physical problem due to which they cannot give birth to their own children, couple can adopt a child or the wife can go through the process of *Niyog* . According to *Manu Smriti*:-

देवराद्धा सपिण्डाद्धा स्त्रिया सम्यड्. नियुक्तया।
प्रजेप्सिताधिगन्तव्या सन्तानस्य परिक्षये।।

A lady, who does not possess children and the reason behind is husband's physical inability or a widow, who is no having any child, can take the permission from Gurus and family head to perform spiritual coalition to give birth to child.

In present environment we can implicit this as if a lady is no capable to conceive because of the physical incapability of husband or in case of a widow of no child, lady can become pregnant by intellectual alliance with a highly spiritual man. I husband is capable while the wife is incapable then they can use proxy womb of a surrogated mother for the birth of a child A lady shall not be cursed for having sexual course with other man to produce a child hence the process of *Niyog* was followed. According to *Manu Smriti*:-

विधवायां नियुक्तस्तु घृताक्तो वाग्यतो निशि ।
एकमुत्पादयेत्पुत्रं न द्वितीयं कथन्चन ॥
द्वितीयमेके प्रजनं मन्यन्ते स्त्रीषु ताद्ददः ।
अनिर्वृतं नियोगार्थं पश्यन्तो धर्मतस्तयोः ॥
विधवायां नियोगार्थं निर्वृते तु यथाविधि ।
गुरूवच्च स्नुषावच्च वर्तयातां परस्परम् ॥
ततः प्रभृति यो मोहात्प्रमीतपतिकां स्त्रियम् ।
नियोजयत्यपत्यार्थं तं निगर्हन्ति साधवः ॥

Thus a childless widow unwilling to remarry or a married lady with no kids because of deficiency in husband may accept a suitable man to get pregnant. Such required man should have perfect control over his senses so that the chastity of himself and of the lady may not get ruined. In this process of *Niyog*, Guru appoints the desired man for such ladies with no child so that he may help them to conceive. In *Niyog* such specific man is chosen who is far away from sensual lust. That man puts Ghee on whole of his body before performing spiritual coalition with that lady. The mental level of such man is so high that not even a single drop of sweat is seen on the body of him and seminal discharge does not occur while the lady becomes pregnant. Thus without coming physically close to each other, they perform sexual association hence the chastity and the elegance of lady is not spoiled. A lady desiring for two children can go through this process done with different men and the reason behind is that a lady performing *Niyog* with a man may keep feeling of sensual lust for that man and may break the rules of *Niyog*

151

during the second time by performing physical interaction with him. After the completion of the sacred process of *Niyog*, the lady and that specific man never come even in the view of each other as this is sternly forbidden in the similar way as a daughter in law is restricted to come in front of her father in law with uncovered face. Though the *Niyog* process is done for the welfare of the widow not willing to remarry so that she may not be *Sati* in the reminiscence of the sad demise of her loving husband and may not commit harlotry but still the people who help in this process are blamed every where. It is not possible to produce a child or conceiving of ladies by such spiritual process in *Kaliyug* hence the process has been ended. In the present time neither of such highly spiritual men are available nor the husband devotee ladies with purity of character and conduct. In the present, the process of *Niyog* became the subject of wonder and ridicule for people belonging to some unauthentic religions.

# <u>Remarriage</u>

Direction of *Manu Smriti* to men and women in context of remarriage are as follows:-

वन्ध्याष्टमेऽधिवेद्याब्दे दशमे तु मृतप्रजा।
एकादशे स्त्रीजननी सद्यस्त्वप्रियवादिनी ।।
या रोगिणी स्यात्तु हिता सम्पन्ना चैव शीलता।
सानुज्ञाप्याधिवेत्तव्या नावमान्या कर्हिचित् ।।
अधिवित्रा तु या नारी निर्गच्छेद्दूषिता गृहात्।
सा सद्यः संनिरो'द्व्या त्याज्या वा कुलसन्निधौ ।।
प्रोषितो धर्मकार्यार्थं प्रतीक्ष्योऽष्टौ नरः समाः।
विद्यार्थं षट् यशोऽर्थं वा कामार्थं त्रींस्तु वत्सरान् ।।

If a lady is barren or not able to conceive within the seven years after the first unsafe period of menstruation cycle from the marriage, up to the eighth year from marriage of her she gives birth to children who dies in few months or years, gives birth to only girl child up to the tenth year from marriage and is not having a son up to the eleventh year from the marriage, husband of her can remarry for the sake of a male child. If a wife is husband devotee but is suffering from some incurable disease and is not able to conceive due to lack of sexual willingness or physical inability then husband to such a lady should nor scold or blame her and should take permission from her in order to remarrying for child. A lady who is of rustic nature, rude behavior, harsh speaking, not worthy to maintain the dignity of the family in any sense,

153

physically incapable to conceive and is involved in illicit sexual relations with other men, if performs harlotry and creates problems on the remarriage of husband then she should be left at her father's place or should be locked inside the room.

If a person has gone to a place of pilgrimage or out of country due to some religious purpose then wife should wait for eight years. If husband has gone out for getting higher education then his wife should wait for him up to six years. If he has gone out to earn the living then wife should wait for three years. A lady is free to remarry if her husband is not back during the above mentioned period depending on the purpose of visit. In *Agni Puran*, following instructions are given to women regarding remarriage:-

नष्टे मृते प्रव्रजिते क्लीबे च पतिते पतौ ।
पञ्चस्वापत्सु नारीणां पतिरन्यो विधीयते ।
मृते तु देवरे देया तदभावे यथेच्छया ॥

If husband is not following the religion, not performing his duties for the family, suddenly dies, renounces the family life by being an ascetic, sexually impotent and is involved in debauchery, wife has the right to remarry. After the demise of the husband, wife should prefer to marry her husband's eligible younger brother if available otherwise she should choose any unmarried man or widower of her preference.

# *Sati Pratha*

The past has illustrated number of examples in the form of history where after the death of husband, wife also suicides by burning herself either in the pyre made for the funeral of her husband or in a new pyre made especially for herself. In some cases known to present, when husbands were assassinated in war and the dead bodies of them were not brought back, their wives accepted death by making their own pyre for burning themselves alive. This way of suicide by burning alive of herself by a lady in a pyre was termed as being *Sati* or being the extreme husband devotee. Mere touching a flame for few moments is painful still widow ladies burn their whole body in the fire without quitting, even on experiencing the extreme pain. Ladies with very strong determination and commendable disposition could take such stern decision. In very ancient period of *Satyug* and *Tretayug*, people were of very high moral and virtuous attributes hence they had a clear communication with the almighty, as a mercy bestowed upon them by God. People worshipped God without desires or being altruistic and God too came into view to help out them on their needs. On the unexpected demise of a husband because of the destiny, the wife used to compel God for the revival of her husband by being *Sati* thereby sacrificing her own life. Mortality was the only difference between the human and the deity because all people were of very virtuous attributes. Thus a lady who performed *Sati* neither felt pain in this activity nor her life came to an end; instead the couple achieved the form of divinity because of this extreme sacrifice done by wife. In *Mahabharat*, the conversation between *Yam* the lord of death and *Savitri* is described as following way:-

निवर्त गच्छ सावित्रि कुरुष्वास्यौर्ध्वदेहिकम् ।
कृतं भर्तुस्त्वयाऽऽनृण्यं यावद् गम्यं गतं त्वया ॥
यत्र में नीयते भर्ता स्वयं वा यत्र गच्छति ।
मया च तत्र गन्तव्यमेष धर्मः सनातनः ॥

Yam says to *Savitri*, "your husband *Satyawan* has died hence now you are free from the responsibilities towards him. In this earth, a wife should perform her duties for husband till the time one of them or both dies."

*Savitri* says, "Wherever you will take the soul of my husband, I shall follow you or you make me dead so that my soul may follow my husband's soul because such dedication for the duties in a chaste woman for a righteous husband is the base of the integrity of the Hindu religion." The request of *Savitri* to *Yam* is described in the *Matsya Puran* in the following way:-

नीयते यत्र भर्ता में स्वयं वा यत्र गच्छति ।
मयाऽपि तत्र गन्तव्यं यथाशक्ति सुरोत्तम ॥
पतिमादाय गच्छन्तमनुगन्तुमहं यदा ।
त्वां देव न हि शक्ष्यामि तदा त्यक्ष्यामि जीवितम् ॥

*Savitri* request to yam "wherever my husband goes or is bound to go I too shall go there. You are taking the soul of my husband so if I would be unable to follow you I shall accept death." *Yam* blessed her and asked her for granting number of boons except the revival of her husband. She cleverly requested for being the mother of children as a blessing hence *Yam* had to resuscitate *Satyawan*.

The examples of *Sati* were also found in the medieval period and even after that. *Sati*, which was considered to be an extreme virtuous sacrifice, came to be known as *Sati Pratha* or the custom of being *Sati* in future. As an upright deed or sacrifice has nothing to do with the self-centeredness while a custom is always somewhere associated with self benefit. Thus the difference started coming in the objectives of being *Sati*. On the martyrdom of Hindu shoulders in war, their wives were forcibly captured by the unbeliever enemies who abhor idol worshipping. Such enemies following other pseudo religion captured the Hindu ladies and forced for prostitution or made concubines just to calm down their religious frustration and impotency. Thus ladies with self respect and virtuous attributes protected themselves from perverted enemies by being *Sati* and established it as *Sati* custom. In such type of cases the enemies were mostly emperor belonging to Islamic despotism. In *Bhavishya Puran*, the reasons for becoming *Sati* are described as following:-

सतीत्वे प्रायशः स्त्रीणां प्रदृष्टं कारणत्रयम् ।
परपुंसामसम्प्रीतिः प्रिये प्रीतिः स्वरक्षणे ।।

Lady who performs *Sati* after the death of her husband has any out of the three reasons behind this, which are difficulty to attain sexual contentment in future, ultimate mental and physical adoration for husband and to protect herself from getting incarcerated for the purpose of sexual molestation or prostitution by the men of different religions. In *Brahama Puran*, the lady who decides to get *Sati* after the death of husband is instructed in the following ways:-

स्त्रीणामयं परो धर्मो यद्भर्तुरनुवेशनम् ।
वेदे च विहितो मार्गः सर्वलोकेषु पूजितः ।
व्यालग्राही यथा व्यालं बिलादुद्धरते बलात् ।
एवं त्वनुगता नारी सह भर्त्रा दिवं व्रजेत् ।।
तिस्रः कोटयोऽर्धकोटी च यानि रोमाणि मानुषे ।
तावत्कालं वसेत्स्वर्गे भर्तारं याऽनुगच्छति ।।

Performing virtuous duties along with the husband is the absolute religion of wife. A husband devotee lady or the one, who performs *Sati*, makes herself and her husband out from all the sins, troubles and misfortune in this world as well as in the other world in the similar way as a snake charmer takes a snake out of hole. A lady, who performs sati, achieves the status of a deity. Being *Sati* after the demise of husband means fulfilling all the duties or performing the family obligations left by husband. Even according to *Manu Sanhita* performing the *Sati* does not denote any kind of physically harming or suicide instead it means to fulfill the rest of the family responsibilities affiliated to the divine relationship with husband after his death.

# Provision of Hell

The provision of heaven and hell was kept to defend people from committing even misdemeanor and to evoke the fortitude in them for performing upright activities. In the early period of *Satyug* and *Tretayug*, people got paradise with the living body due to their extreme noble conduct and virtuous deeds but gradually in future the graph of this went down. In *KaliYug*, the imagination to occupy paradise for people either in living stage or after death in the other world was futile. People who were involved into the sins, had to go to hell after death, and this assumption is still believed. According to holy religious saying, person who commits even a single peccadillo in his life time is destined to go to hell. Twenty eight kinds of hells are described in the following ways in *Devi Bhagwat Mahapuran*:-

तामिस्र अन्धतामिस्रो रौरवोऽपि तृतीयकः ।
महारौरवनामा च कुम्भीपाकोऽपरो मतः ।।
कालसूत्रं तथा चाऽसिपत्रारण्यमुदाहृतम् ।
सूकरस्य मुखं चान्धकूपोऽथ कृमिभोजनः ।
संदंशस्तप्तमूर्तिश्च वज्रकण्टक एव च ।
शाल्मली चाऽथ देवर्षे! नाम्ना वैतरणी तथा ।।
पूयोदः प्राणरोधश्च तथा विशसनं मतम् ।
लालाभक्षः सारमेयादनमुक्तमतः परम् ।।
अवीचिरप्ययः पानं क्षारकर्दम एवं च ।

रक्षोगणाख्यसम्भोज: शूलप्रोतोऽप्यत: परम् ।।
दन्दशूकोऽवटारोध: पर्यावर्तनक: परम् ।
सूचीमुखमिति प्रोक्ता अष्टाविंशतिनारका: ।।

Tamisra, Andhtamisra, Raurav, Maharaurav, Kumbhipak, Kalsutra, Asipatraven, Sukarmukh, Andhkup, KrimiBhojan, Sandansh, Taptmurti, Vajrakantak, Shalmali, Vatarani, Puyod or Pranroadh, Vishsan, Lalabhaksh, Sarmeyaden, Arichi or, Ayaha Pan, Sharkardam, Rakshogan, Sambhojan, Shoolproat, Dandshuk, Avatarodh, Paryavartan and Suchimukh are the twenty eight kinds of hells occupied by the human to get punished on the basis of the awful activities they perform in their life time.

If a man kidnaps another's wife or allures her so that she absconds from the camaraderie of her husband to settle with that man then he has to face the hell termed as Tamisra, If a man carries sexual associations with a married lady thereby making her an adulteress then such person has to face up the hell after death termed as Andhtamisra. A lady or a man when keeps sexually coalition with a partner who is Agamya, a person with which they are sternly forbidden to keep sexual relations as per the directions stipulated by the religion, occupies the hell after death termed as Taptsurmi, where they are whipped. The sexually perverted people, who perform unnatural sexual mating with animals, go to Shalmali hell. Men who keep illicit sexual relations with other's wife or ladies who keep such illegitimate sexual relations with other's

161

husband face the fire of *Shukrakund* hell after death. One who gives birth to a girl child and then sells her at beginning or at the time of her marriage by taking money or any other kind of benefit from her husband or from any other person, goes to *Maskund* hell. A man performing sexual intercourse with a pregnant lady goes to *Tamrakund* hell. A man who sexually intercourses with a lady having number of husbands or intakes the supper provided by such lady occupies *Kalsutra* hell. The man, who kills a lady by mistake or by conspiracy occupies *Raurav* hell and endures severe physical pain. In *Devi Bhagwat Mahapuran*, the above punishments are described in the following way:-

अयस्मयैरग्निपिण्डैः सन्दंशैर्निष्कुषन्ति च।
योऽगम्या योषितं गच्छेदगभ्यं पुरुषं च या ॥
तावमुत्रापि कशया ताड्यन्तो यमानुगाः तिग्मया।
लोहमय्या च सूर्म्याऽऽलिंगगयन्ति तम् ॥
ताश्चापि योषितं सूर्म्याऽऽलिंगयन्ति यमानुगाः।
यस्तु सर्वाभिगमनः पुरुषः पापसंचयी ॥
निरयेऽमुत्र तं याम्याः शाल्मलीं रोपयन्ति तम्।

— — — — — — — — — — — — — — —

यो वै परस्य वित्तानि दारापत्यानि चैव हि।
हरते स हि दुष्टात्मा यमानुचरगोचरः ॥
कालापाशेन सम्बद्धो याम्यैरतिभयानकैः।
तामिस्रनामनरके पात्यते यातनास्पदे ॥
यः पतिं वन्चयित्वा तु दारादीनुपभुज्यति।

अन्धतामिस्त्रनरके पात्यते यमकिङ्करैः ।
पुरुषो यः स्त्रियं हन्याज्ज्ञानतोऽज्ञानतोऽपि वा ।
नरके पच्यते सोऽथ महारौरवपूर्वके ।।

It is said that the man who performs illicit sexual union with other's lady or *Agamya* and the lady who performs adultery with other's man, are send to hell named as *Taptasurmi*. Such debauchees are whipped in the passage and are compelled to embrace hot burning statue of opposite gender. Whoever keeps abnormal sexual relations with animals is send to hell termed as *Shalmali*. Whoever abducts a lady or money or progeny of others is send to deep hell by the cohort of the lord of death and is brutally beaten by sticks. At that moment, the soul of such person repents about the misdeeds committed in human life. Whoever performs adultery with an unmarried one for the sake of sexual pleasure or money is send to hell named as *Andhtamishra*.

Again in context of the type of hells provided as a punishment on committing misdeeds regarding women, *Shiv Puran* states the following verses:-

योषितांजारसक्तानांनरकेयमकिङ्कराः ।।
संतप्तलो हपरिघं क्षिपन्तिस्मरमन्दिरे ।।
नवयौ वनमत्ताश्च मर्या दाभेदिनश्च ये ।।
ते कृत्वं यान्त्यशौचाश्च कुलकार्जीविनश्च ये ।।
साध्वया विक्रयकृश्चाथ वार्द्धकी केशविक्रयी ।।
तप्तलोहेषु पच्यते यश्च भक्तं परित्यजेत् ।।

163

An adulteress or a married lady, who sexually intercourses with other man than her husband, is chastised in the hell where the follower of *Yum*, the lord of death and punishment, physically torture her by putting the hot iron rod through her vagina. People who loose their senses and break the code of conduct by involving in debauchment and who earn their living by depending upon a lady, occupy *kritya* hell. A man, who sells a chaste lady, sells the hair or modesty of virtuous ladies and earns by money-lending, goes to hell named as *Taptlauha*.

# Punishments on Offenses

The criterion of punishment for men is more severe comparatively to women. According to *Manu Smriti*, the penalties imposed on the people involved in the crimes related to women are the following:-

अकन्येति तु यः कन्यां ब्रूयाद् द्वेषेण मानवः ।
स शतं प्राप्नुयाद्दण्डं तस्या दोषमदर्शयन् ॥
योऽकामां दूषयेत्कन्यां स सद्यो वधमर्हति ।
सकामां दूषयंस्तुल्यो न वधं प्राप्नुयात्तरः ॥
अभिषंका तु यः कन्यां कुर्याद्दर्पेण मानवः ।
तस्याशु कर्त्ये अंगुल्यौ दण्डं चार्हति षट्शतम् ॥
सकामां दूषयंस्तुल्यो नांगुलिच्छेदमानुयात् ।
द्विशतं तु दमं दाप्यः प्रसंगविनिवृतये ॥
कन्यैव कन्यां या कुर्याश्चास्याः स्याद् द्विशतो दमः ।
शुल्कं च द्विगुणं दद्याच्छिफौवान्नुयाद् दंश ॥
या तु कन्यां प्रकुर्यात् स्त्री सा सद्यो मौड.यमर्हति ।
अंगुल्योरेव वा छेदं खरेणोद्वहनं तथा ॥
भर्तारं लंघयेद्या तु स्त्री ज्ञातिगुणदर्पिता ।
तां द्विभिः खादयेद्राजा संस्थाने बहुसंस्थिते ॥
पुमांसं दाहयेत्पापं शयने तप्त आयसे ।
अभ्यादध्यु च काष्ठानि तत्र दह्येत पापकृत ॥
न माता न पिता न स्त्री पुत्रस्त्यागमर्हति ।
त्यज्यापतितानेतान् राजा दण्डयः शतानि षट् ॥
परस्त्रियं योऽभिवदेतीर्थेऽरण्ये वनेऽपि वा ।
नदीनां वाऽपि संभेदे स संग्रहणमानुयात् ॥
परदाराभिमर्शेषु प्रवृश्चान्महीपतिः ।
उद्वेजनकरैर्दण्डैश्छित्वायिता प्रवासयेत् ॥

165

If any one speaks ill about the virginity of a girl of virtuous conduct, in-between the other people just for the sake of achieving perverted sexual pleasure or to falsely blame her should be punished by king of the regime. If a person becomes morally corrupt and sexually rapes a noble lady thereby breaking her virginity, should be killed without any delay by the order of king but if it seems that the lady too was willing to have sexual fun then he should not be punished. If a person forcefully breaks the virgin knot or hymen of an unconscious or conscious girl by putting his finger or an object other than penis in her vagina then he is culprit and should be punished by some financial charge and his tow fingers should be cut. If the girl supports him in such shameful deed then he should be punished by heavy financial charge so that in future he may not repeat the same act even on the consent of a girl. If an offender virgin girl performs the act to rupture the virgin knot or hymen of the other virgin girl then the culprit first girl has to pay money as a fine to king as well as double the amount of that money to the other girl whose virginity she tried to break artificially by putting the fingers or other object in her vagina and further she should be whipped ten times. If a lady does the same mischievous act with a virgin girl then all her hair would be shaven out or two fingers would be cut or she would have to ride blacken face on an ass publicly. If any lady shows arrogance on her father's prosperity and power thereby disrespects and abuses her husband, should be scratched by dogs publicly. If a man is found to be involved in debauchment hence keeps illicit sexual relations with other ladies then he should be laid on the hot iron bed and burning wooden blocks should be kept upon him so that he may burn in to ashes. If a man leaves his parents, devotee and virtuous wife and a minor child then he would have to face a financial retribution. If a man is found having any type of sexual conversation with other lady at the place of pilgrimage, near to river, in a forest or garden and at the bank of river then he would have to pay fine. If a man is found having sexual relations forcefully with other's lady without her consent then he would have to bare physical punishment and his ear-nose would be cut and would have to go on an exile.

प्रकाशं वाऽप्रकाशं व मन्युस्तं मन्युमृच्छति ।
गृहक्षेत्राभिहर्तारस्तथाऽगम्याभिगामिनः ।।
भिक्षुकोऽप्यथवा नारी योऽपि वा स्यात्कुशीलवः ।।
प्रविशेत्प्रतिषिद्धस्तु प्राप्नुयाद्द्विगुणं दम ।
परस्त्रीणां तु संभाषे तीर्थऽरण्ये गृहेऽपि वा ।।
नदीनां चैव संभेदे स संग्रहणमाप्नुयात् ।
न संभाषेतपरस्त्रीभिः प्रतिषिद्धः समाचरेत् ।।
प्रतिषिद्धे समाभाष्य सुवर्ण दण्डमर्हति ।

- - - - - - - - - -

प्रेष्यासु चैव सर्वासु गृहप्रव्रजितासु च ।
योऽकामां दूषयेत्कन्यां स सद्यो वधमर्हति ।।

सकामां दूषयाणस्तु प्राप्नुयादि्द्विशतं दमम् ।
यश्च संरक्षकस्तत्र पुरूषः स तथा भवेत् ।।
पारदारिकवद्दण्ड्यो योऽपि स्यादवकाशदः ।
बलात्संदूषयेद्यस्तु परभार्या नरः क्वचित् ।।

वधो दण्डो भवेत्तस्य नापराधो भवेत्त्रियाः ।।

The severity of an offense and the penalty imposed for
that is same whether it is perpetrated clandestinely in the dark
of the night or publicly in the day time. If a person is found to
be involved in unauthentic seizing of other's residence
kidnapping other's woman and committing sexual intercourse
with *Agamaya* lady then he has to go through punishment. If a
beggar, other woman, bards and minstrels enter the house
even when they have been warned for not doing so then they
are eligible for punishment. If a man is found talking to other
ladies with malicious intentions then he has to face the
punishment and if even after warning, he repeats the same
activity then he has to pay the fine of gold. This punishment is
also applicable on maid servants of the house if they try to talk
unnecessarily to the men of the house. If a man sexually
intercourses with a virgin or minor girl then he should be given
severe punishment as death sentence and the owner of the
place, where that misdeed is done, should also be punished. If
a man compellingly keeps sexual relations with other's wife
thus molests her chastity then he should be killed immediately
but if it is found that the married lady supported him in doing

168

so then he should not be punished. The criteria of punishments mentioned in *Mahabharat* are as following:-

गुरूतल्पमधिष्ठाय दुरात्मा पापचेतनः।
स्त्रयाकारां प्रतिमां लिंग्य मृत्युना सोऽभिशुद्ध्यति।।

— — — — — — — — — — — — —

अथवा शिश्नवृषणावादायान्जलिना स्वयम्।।
एवं तु समभिज्ञातामात्रेयीं वा निपातयेत्।।
द्विगुणा ब्रह्महत्या वै आत्रेयीनिघने भवेत्।
पुमांसमुन्नयेत् प्राज्ञः शयने तप्त आयसे।
अप्यादधीत दारूणि तत्र दह्येत पापकृत्।।
एष दण्डो महाराज स्त्रीणां भर्तृष्यतिक्रमात्।
भार्यायां व्यभिचारिण्यां निरूद्धायां विशेषतः।
यत् पुंसः परदारेषु तदेनां चारयेद् व्रतम्।।
श्रेयांसं शयनं हित्वा यान्यं पापं निगच्छति।
श्रवभिस्तामर्दयेद् राजा संस्थाने बहुविस्तरे।।

A man of perverted malicious thoughts if involved in illicit sexual relations with his Guru's wife then he should embrace an extremely heated iron statue of woman thereby committing suicide or else he should cut his penis and scrotum to save himself from punishment. A person who kills a pregnant lady is liable for the punishment for the death of two saints because a lady is considered to be utterly praiseworthy in the time of her pregnancy. A person who is involved in illicit sexual relations should be laid between bed of hot iron and burning wooden block so that he could die with

169

the heat of fire and burn to ashes. The same punishment is applicable on women who commit harlotry or found to be living a life of debauchery. If a lady is involved in illicit sexual relation and is caught red handed then she has to perform the same way of repent as applicable for the man. If a lady divorces his noble character husband and keeps sexual relations with other man then the king should punish such harlot by making her scratched by dogs publicly till she dies.

# Payment of debt

Following are the verses from *Agni Puran* in context of payment of debt:-

ऋक्थग्राह ऋणं दाप्यो योषिद्ग्रहस्तथैव च।

– – – – – – – – – – – – – – – –

न योषित् पतिपुत्राभ्यां न पुत्रेण कृतं पिता।
दद्यादृते कुटुम्बार्थात्र पतिः स्त्रीकृतं तथा॥
प्रतिपन्नं स्त्रियां देयं पत्या वा सह यत् कृतप्।
स्वयं कृतं वा यदृणं नान्यस्त्री दातुमर्हति॥

If a man marries a widow or a wife of other man then the debt of that lady is paid by second husband. A wife is not obligated to disburse the debt taken by husband. Similarly the parents are not accountable for the liabilities taken by son. If a wife takes the debt for the accomplishment of sensual enjoyment of herself then husband in not compelled to pay the debt but if the debt is taken by her for the welfare of the family then husband in liable to pay back. If the wife has taken the debt then she herself has to pay off it when the husband dies. If the loan in taken by husband for the welfare of the family and is utilized appropriately then on the demise of him, it is the duty of wife to pay if she is enough capable to pay it back. Except this, a lady is not bound to pay any kind of debt.

171

# Medieval Period-*Brahtahari Satak-Chanakya Neet*

To perceive the ethical and depraved persona of ladies of the medieval period, the *Sringar Satak* and *Vairagya Satak* written by the great king *Brahtahari* are sufficient. The palace of king *Brahtahari* was situated in *Ujjainiy* city of *Malwa* which is presently known as *Ujjain*. The king *Brahtahari* was the elder brother of lord *Vikramaditya* and was a king of justice. The king, even being an extraordinary man of discretion and ethics, was intensely enthralled by her gorgeous younges wife, queen *Pingala*. There was a saint in the regime of the king who involved in vigorous meditation. God blessed him with a fruit and instructed that whoever will eat it, will become ever young and physically immortal. Saint thought that by eating the fruit, his poverty was not going to end, thus he decided to give that fruit to great king *Brahtahari* and get some money as a reward. He gifted that fruit to king by telling him about the special feature of it and took a lot of money as an award. King immensely fascinated by *Pingala*, gifted that frui to her in the night so that she remains young forever. King told her the miraculous feature of the fruit then she replied that she would eat it after taking bath in the next morning. In fact king's most lovable and trustworthy wife *Pingala* was of il character and was involved in illicit sexual relations with a groom of the city who was also appointed to take care of the horses of the king. In the morning, when king left for his royal court, adulteress queen did sexual intercourse with that groom and gave him the fruit with a thought that if he would eat it, he could always satisfy the ever unsatisfied sexual need of her. That groom visited every night to a specific prostitute of the city and was in love with her. On the next night, he gifted divine fruit to that harlot so that she may remain ever beautiful. After the sexual mating with the groom, when he left, she decided to eat that fruit. She had heard the quality of divine fruit and the moment she became alone, her conscience evoked. She thought that after eating fruit she will be blessed to be ever young but she will remain a prostitute hence the quality of making immortal will become a curse for her. She decided to give that fruit to king *Brahtahari*. That prostitute gifted the fruit to king publicly and told him the quality of it. Receiving the same fruit from a prostitute, which he gave to his wife *Pingala*, opened the door of knowledge to him and he came to know that there was a man in between that prostitute and queen *Pingala* and both of them have illicit sexual relations with him. With this thought, he left his throne and queen *Pingala* forever and become an ascetic. The sexual character of lady is expressed in the *Sringar Satak* written by king *Brahtahari*. It also depicts how the man relinquishes morel attributes and scruples hence gets diverted from the virtuous track of worshipping God and gets mentally as well as

physically engaged in endeavors to acquire a woman body for
sexual pleasure.

स्मितेन भावेन च लज्जया भिया पराङ्मुखैरर्द्ध कटाक्ष वीक्षणैः।
वचोभिरीर्ष्या कलहेन लीलया समस्त भावैः खलु बन्धनं स्त्रियः॥
भ्रू चातुर्यात्कुञ्चिताक्षाः कटाक्षाः स्निग्धा वाचो लज्जितान्ताश्च
हासाः।
लीलामन्दं प्रस्थितं च स्थितं च स्त्रीणामेतद् भूषणं चायुधं च॥
वक्त्रं चंद्रविकासि पङ्कजपरिहासक्षमे लोचने वर्णः
स्वर्णमपाकरिष्णुरलिनीजिष्णुः कचानांचयः।
वक्षोजाविभकुंभविभ्रमहरौ गुर्वी नितम्बस्थली वाचां हारि च मार्दवं
युवतिषु स्वाभाविकं मण्डनम्॥
सम्मोह्यन्ति मदयन्ति विडम्बयन्ति निभर्त्सयन्ति रमयन्ति
विषादयन्ति।
एताः प्रविश्य सदयं हृदयं नराणाम् किं नाम वामनयना न
समाचरन्ति॥
संसारेऽस्मिन्नसारे परिणतितरले द्वे गती पण्डितानां
तत्त्वज्ञानामृताम्भः प्लवललितधियां यातु कालः कदाचित्।
नो चेन्मुग्धांगनानां स्तनजघनघना भोगसम्भोनिनीनां
स्थूलोपस्थस्थलीषु स्थगितकरतलस्पर्शलीलोद्यतानाम्॥
प्राङ्मामेति मनागनागतरसं जाताभिलाषं ततः सव्रीडं
तदनुश्लथीकृततनुः प्रध्वस्तधैर्यं पुनः।
प्रेमार्द्रे स्पृहणीयनिर्भररहः क्रीडाप्रगल्भं ततो
निश्शङ्कंगविकर्षणाधिकसुखं रम्यं कुलस्त्रीरतम्॥
मालती शिरसि जृम्भणोन्मुखी चन्दनं वपुषि कुंकुमान्वितम्।
वक्षसि प्रियतमा मदालसा स्वर्ग एव परिशिष्ट आगतः॥
आमीलितनयनानां यः सुरतरसोऽनुसंविद् कुरूते।
मिथुनैर्मिथोऽवधारितमवितथमिदमेव कामनिर्वहणम्॥
इदमनुचितमक्रमश्च पुंसां यदिह जरास्वपि मान्मथाः विकाराः।
तदपि च न कृतं नितम्बिनीनां स्तनपतनावधि जीवितं रतं वा॥

आवासः क्रियतां गंगे पापहारिणी वारिणि ।
स्तनद्वये तरुण्या वा मनोहारिणी हारिणी ।।
किमिह बहुभिरुक्तैर्युक्तिशून्यैः प्रलापैर्द्वयमिह पुरुषाणां सर्वदा
सेवनीयम् ।
अभिनवमदलीलालालसं सुन्दरीणाम् स्तनभरपरिखिन्नं यौवनं वा
वनं वा ।।
सत्यं जना वच्मि न पक्षणताल्लोकेषु सप्तस्वपि तथ्यमेतत् ।
नान्यन्मनोहारि नितम्बिनीभ्यो दुःखैकहेतुर्न च कश्चिदन्यः ।।
उन्मत्तप्रेमसंरम्भादारभन्ते यदंगनाः ।
तत्र प्रत्यूहमाधातुं ब्रह्मापि खलु कातरः ।।

According to *Bhratahari*, ladies trap men in the snares of illusion and sensual lust by expressing a sweet and innocent smile, indecent gestures provoking sexual perversion, expressing artificial or pseudo coyness, making an eye contact and then suddenly casting from sight pretending to be frightened from the society, the rhythmic combination of flirtatious glance with melodious voice and showing possessiveness with jealousy. Pretending bashfulness during easy conversation and verbal enjoyment, walking unnecessarily but in a beautiful looking way by giving flirtatious and rhythmic movement to buttocks and trying to attract men by looking them with a sidelong glance are the natural jewels and important weapons of the arsenal of women to sexually seduce men. The appealing sensual properties of a lady like having an attractive face with glory of moon, beautiful eyes more gorgeous than petals of lotus, young body shining like gold, providing delusion to beetles by their long black hair, heavy and well shaped breast, bulky and attractive buttocks and the art of pleasant speaking, are considered to be her natural beguiling qualities and cannot be invoked artificially. Ladies vanishes the power of prudence of men by their beauty and sex-appeal. When they are proposed for love by men, they express sincerity on face but behind the back, they laugh on them. Ladies criticize men if they try to touch them while on invoking the sexual desire in themselves, they become ready to perform sexual intercourse without delay. The moment they are sexually satisfied, they blame, for their sexual harassment, to the mating partners deceitfully and even betray them. Thus ladies always make a soft corner in the hearts of men by acting as their fiancée thereby absorbing everything from them. According to *Brahtahari*, to meditate or worship God keeping sensual lust for women is futile and similarly it make no sense for a man of ethics and conscience getting effected by sexual appeal of women. Thus a man has only two possible ways of life in this mortal and unpredictable world, either he should fully devote himself in praying to God or he should ignore the existence of God and utilize his time with naked women of attractive thigh, buttocks and heavy breast with peaky nipples by rubbing their vagina in order to excite them for sexual intercourse. A lady always allures desired man for the sexual intercourse but initially due to having partial sexual excitement, she denies to perform mating on touching by that man. The moment of getting

176

frenzied of love, she looses her body by leaving control over her organs thereby showing artificial introversion by her gestures and then gives acquiescence for sexual coalition. At that moment, she no more hinders man from removing her clothes instead on stirring up of passion, she plays the game of sexual delight and enjoys in it. To embrace a lady, who puts fragranced garland of flowers on the hair tied up behind and perfumed lotions on the body, provides the gratification of heaven to a man of no discernment. After the sexual union, man and woman hug each other, close their eyes and take pleasure in the satisfaction. The sexual coalition is said to be significant and successful only when both of man and woman satisfies each other's sexual desire.

According to *Brahtahari*, there is no constraint kept upon the passion of love on the basis of age or physical stage of human and hankering for sexual pleasure troubles in the old age also hence God has done this big injustice to man kind. Ladies are also troubled by the same as such craving for sensual contentment not ends in them even when they become overage and the shape as well as beauty of their breasts and other organs vanishes. He says that a man should not accept the mid way hence either he should build a small cottage in front of the great river *Ganga*, which eradicates the awful outcome of unethical deeds committed by human being, and live their being an ascetic or he should keep his mouth at the valley between the two breasts of a stripped lady with necklace of pearls and experience sexual pleasure. Again it is directed that men should stay away from the useless talks and futile activities and should concentrate on either of the following deeds. Such deeds are either become a saint and renounce the world or to sexually intercourse with ladies of heavy breast, in different postures. He further instructs to lustful men as "Friends! I without any partiality, announce that in all the seven possible worlds in the universe, no satisfaction is greater than the satisfaction that is achieved in having sexual mating with a lady of heavy and fleshy breast and buttocks but this is also true that ladies are the only cause of every disaster and trouble in a man's life". Ladies agitated because of passion of love create delusion of actual love to allure men to get sexual reconciliation and are always succeeded in such efforts because even almighty God is incapable to endow with conscience and wisdom to a lady who is stirring up of passion.

King *Brahtahari* realized the veracity of ladies in future and wrote *Vairagya Satak* which is considered to be an extraordinary incomparable collection. King *Brahtahari* accepted that if a man is not able to satisfy the sexual need of a lady, then he is not worthy of being a man in that lady's view. In *Sri Narsingh Puran*, it is said in context of the definition of manliness or masculinity of men in the views of women that तद्यौवनं यद्युवतीविनोदो means according to the opinion of a lady, only that man is worthy to be said as a complete man who satisfies the endless sexual need of her and sexually entertains her.

In *Vairagya Satak*, *Brahtahari* warned men regarding the truth of ladies behind their pseudo behavior. Men who are having conscience yet trapped in the pseudo love of ladies are pronounced by following statement said by *Brahtahari*:-

यां चिन्तयामि सततं मयि सा विरक्ता साप्यन्यमिच्छति जनं स जनोऽन्यसक्तः ।
अस्मत्कृते च परिशुष्यति काचिदन्या धिक् तां च तं च मदनं च इमां च मां च ।।

My fiancée, whom I love more than my life, loves another person. Whom she adores, keeps sexual relation with other lady. The lady, who is sexually available to that person, offers her sexual service to me by spreading her arms. Thus, shame to the source of lust or women as well as to the creator of lust or *Kamdeva*.

जल्पन्ति साधमन्येन पश्यन्त्यन्यं सविभ्रमाः ।
हृदये चिन्तयन्त्यन्यं प्रियः को नाम योषिताम् ।।
शास्त्रज्ञोऽपि प्रथितविनयोऽप्यात्मबोधोऽपि बाढम
संसारेऽस्मिन् भवति विरलो भाजनं सद्गतीनाम् ।
येनैतस्मिन् निरयनगरद्वारमुद्घाटयन्ति वामाक्षीणां भवति
कुटिला भ्रूलता कुञ्चिकेव ।।
कान्तेत्युत्पललोचनेति विपुलश्रोणीभरेत्युन्नमत्पीनोतुंगपयोधरेति
सुमुखाम्भोजेति सुभ्रूरिति ।

179

दृष्ट्वा माद्यति मोदतेऽभिरमते प्रस्तौति विद्वानपि
प्रत्यक्षाशुचिभस्त्रिकां स्त्रियमहो मोहस्य दुश्चेष्टितम् ।।

कृशः काणः खञ्जः श्रवणरहितः पुच्छविकलो व्रणी पूयक्लिनः
कृमिकुलशतैरावृततनुः ।
क्षुधाक्षामो जीर्णः पिठरककपालार्पितगलः शुनीमन्वेति श्वा
हतमपि निहन्त्येव मदनः ।।

स्मृता भवति तापाय दृष्टा चोन्मादकारिणी । सृष्टा भवति
मोहाय सा नाम दयिता कथम् ।।

नामृतं न विषं किञ्चिदेतां मुक्त्वा नितम्बिनीम् । सैवामृतलता
रक्ता विरक्ता विषवल्लरी ।।

लीलावतीनां सहजा विलासास्त एव मूढस्य हृदि स्फुरन्ति
रागो नलिन्या हि निसर्गसिद्धस्तत्र भ्रमत्येव वृथा षडड्घ्रिः ।।

आवर्तः संशयानामविनयभवनं पत्तनं साहसाना । दोषाणां
सन्निधानं कपटशतमयं क्षेत्रमप्रत्ययानाम् ।
स्वर्गद्वारस्य विघ्नो नरकपुरमुखं सर्वमायाकरण्डं स्त्रीयन्त्रं
केन सृष्टं विषममृतमयं प्राणिलोकस्य पाशः ।।

सत्येव्वे न शशाङ्क एव वदनीभूतो न चेन्दीवर द्वन्द्वं
लोचनतां गतं न कनकैरप्यंगयष्टिः कृता ।
किन्त्वेवं कविभिः प्रतारितमनस्तत्त्वं विजानन्नपि, त्वङ्
मांसास्थिमयं वपुर्मृगदृशां मन्दो जनः सेवते ।।

मधु तिष्ठति वाचि योषितां, हृदि हालाहलमेव केवलम् ।
अतएव निपीयतेऽधरो, हृदयं मुष्टिभिरेव ताड्यते ।।

व्यादीर्घेण चलेन वक्रगतिना तेजस्विना भोगिना
नीलाब्जद्युतिनाऽहिना वरमहं दष्टो न तच्चक्षुषा ।
दृष्टे सन्ति चिकित्सका दिशिदिशि प्रायेण धर्मार्थिनो ।
मुग्धाक्षीक्षणवीक्षितस्य न हि मे वैद्यो न चाप्यौषधम् ।।

जात्यन्धाय च दुर्मुखाय च जराजीर्णाखिलाङ्गाय च ।

ग्रामीणाय च दुष्कुलाय च गलत्कुष्ठाभिभूताय च ।
यच्छन्तीषु मनोहरं निजवपुर्लक्ष्मीलवश्रद्धया,
पण्यस्त्रीषु विवेककल्पलतिकाशस्त्रीषु रज्येत कः ।।

180

कश्चुम्बति कुलपुरूषो वेश्याधरपल्लवं मनोज्ञमपि।
चारभटचोरचेटकविट-नट-निष्ठीवनशरावम्॥
वेश्यासौ मदनज्वाला रूपेन्धनसमेधिता।
कामिभिर्यत्र हूयन्ते यौवनानि धनानि च॥
विरमत बुधा! योषित्संगात्सुखात्क्षणभंगुरात्
कुरूत करूणामैत्रीप्रज्ञावधूजनसंगमम्।
न खलु नरके हाराक्रान्तं घनस्तनमण्डलं
शरणमथवा श्रोणिबिम्बं रणन्मणिमेखलम्॥
विरहेऽपि संगमः खलु परस्परं संगतं मनो येषाम्।
हृदयमपि विघट्टितं चेत्सङ्गेग विरहं विशेषयति।

A lady does romantic conversations with one man but gives a sidelong glance to allure some other man by rotating her eye balls while thinks about getting sexual pleasure with a third man. Thus, it is not possible for a lady to have sensual affection or love for a single man. A man, who is even well versed with the sense of discernment, does not get free from the cycle of birth and death hence never get rid from committing transgression because beautiful ladies staring men with sexually alluring flirtatious glance are always available in this world to open the door of hell for them.

Men get attracted towards the beauty of ladies, their heavy breasts, sharp eyebrows, heavy buttocks and fleshy thighs and keep the desire of sexual intercourse with them though each of them is well familiar with the fact that ladies are the most impure living being and divert men from the righteous track. Whose remembrance be the cause of anguish, appearance makes a man comatose, touch creates illusion, can never be endearing to anyone. A dog who is physically very lean, mutilated because of missing of some organ of the body, crippled, ugly, dreadfully wounded with pus flowing out, hungry, old and the one whose head is sink and stick in the hole of mud pitcher also runs behind the young bitch moving his tale and poking out the tongue dropping his saliva in order to perform sexual coalition with her. The acts and illusions made by deity *Kamdev* are surprising because he makes a person dead, who is already dead, by dropping him in the deep horrible valley of sexual lust. There is no such other ambrosia available to lusty and immoral men as a young woman and there is no such disastrous poison or curse is available for ascetics and for the people of moral like a young girl.

This is a very normal tendency of ladies to pass little smile and rotate their eye balls here and there while chatting to others. A man who lacks conscience and is dull-witted feels that such ladies are attracted towards him in the same way as when a black beetle looks the natural reddish color of lotus flower, he thinks that the flower is feeling coyness due to his presence and is in love with him but in reality, it naturally possesses reddish color. Ladies always invoke doubts and disorders in men's thinking, show unnecessary stubbornness and evasion, become disposed to spoil any one up to any extent if are annoyed, become the quarry of misdeeds and it

182

intentions if infuriated, tell lie by putting false sexual blames on others and betray when come to take revenge, can not be directed to move on the righteous path if once sidetracked from it, vanish the pious outcomes of the good deeds done by men in their life time, put the men in trouble in this world and in the next world by the snares of sexual illusion made by them, are the gateway to hell for men if not sexually satisfied, utilize the shrewdness governed by women psychology to ruin one's life if dislike him and appear to be pleasant as holy water but in fact are more dangerous than deadly poison. Whoever created these women, has put the men in the horrible valley of hell.

In reality, the face of a woman is not made by moon, neither her eyes are made out of lotus petals nor even her body is made of gold. Due to the exaggeration done by poets, man wants to live in the propinquity of women, who are actually made of bones, flesh and blood. The lips of ladies are just like honey while their breast or heart is full of poison. This is the reason why lips of ladies are kissed and breasts are pressed by men.

*Brahtahari* says that it is fine to be bitten by a long, furious and poisonous snake rather being trapped in the delusion of love of a beautiful lady because the bite of snake is curable but a man ditched by the lady can never get cured. Ladies get ready for sexual intercourse the moment they get frenzy of love or for the sake of money, with even a man who is blind by birth, ugly looking, with no discretion or is bovine physically lean, suffering from leprosy and hatred. A man of prudence should not get attracted towards such kind of ladies having tendency to kill like a sword. A man of morals can not kiss the beautiful looking lips of a morally polluted lady, which are in fact like a spittoon where men of no gravity, thieves pimp of prostitutes, professional folk dancers and singers of Muslim community, jugglers, acrobats, procurers, conjurers spits by kissing.

According to *Brahtahari,* prostitutes are such fire of sexual passion which gets satisfaction only by burning beauty adolescence, manliness, health and prosperity of men. A men should keep sagacity, mercy and universal sodality for human being and accept the bare veracity of women, hence should not get diverted towards the momentary pleasure of sexual intercourse because persons involved in illicit sexual activities, occupies hell after death and there no ladies with heavy breasts shall wait to accompany them.

In context of actual love, king *Brahtahari* says that male-female pair, where partners perform spiritual love and are of unadulterated feelings or soul thereby act according to each other's welfare, live always near to each other even when they are not physically close and the partners who do not believe in such kind of spiritual love and always involve in sexual relations, never get close to each other even after being in each other's arms.

Sage *Chanakya* is considered to be the historical master of the politics. According to him:-

जल्पन्ति सार्धमन्येन पश्यन्त्यं सविभ्रमाः ।
हृदये चिन्तयन्त्यन्यं न स्त्रीणामेकतो रतिः ।।
यो मोहान्मन्यते मूढो रक्तेयं मयि कामिनी ।
स तस्य वशगो भूत्वा नृत्येत क्रीडा-शकुन्तवत ।।

While performing love conversation with a man, ladies look with enticing view to other man to allure him sexually and at the same instant they keep romantic thoughts of sexual union with some third man. Thus no man can stay alone as a fiancé in the heart of a woman because women can never be sexually satisfied with a single partner. Whoever thinks that a lady is in love with him is utter stupid and performs like a bird or an animal tamed by that lady thus follows her instructions and denies the actual duties. *Chanakya* says that:-

अग्निरापः स्त्रियो मूर्खा सर्पा राजकुलानि च ।
नित्यं यत्नेन सेव्यानि सद्यः प्राणहराणि षट ।।

स्त्रीणां द्विगुण आहारो बुद्धिस्तासां चतुर्गुणा ।
साहसं षड्गुणं चैव कामोऽष्टगुण उच्यते ।।

अनृतं साहसं माया मूर्खत्वमतिलुब्धता ।
अशौचत्वं निर्दयत्वं स्त्रीणां दोषाः स्वभावजाः ।।

One should always keep a sufficient distance with fire, water, women, a duffer, snakes and person belonging to a ruling dynasty because all of aforesaid mentioned possess a drawback to cause disaster if kept in close proximity. He says that the hunger for sensual pleasure as well as for food of women is twice of the hunger of men, sagacity is of four times than that of men, audacity is of six times of men and sexual lust or passion for love is eight times than that of men. Here sagacity means tact of betraying and dishonesty while audacity means boldness in committing ill deeds or transgressions. Women by nature are dishonest, ready to perform ill deeds intrepidly, betrayer, shrewd, extreme greedy physically and morally impure and extremely cruel in comparison to men. *Chanakya* specifies the highly reputed role of a mother as:-

मातृवत् परदारश्च

न मातुः परं दैवतम्

One should always consider other's women as his mother and thus respect them. No one is more respectable and praiseworthy for a man than his own mother. *Chanakya* says that:-

स्त्रीभ्यः शिक्षेत् कैतवम्

भार्या रुपवती शत्रुः

सलज्जा गणिका नष्टा निर्लज्जाश्च कुलांगना ।।

वरं न दारा न कुदारदाराः

जारस्त्रीणां पतिः शत्रु

Politicians should learn the way of making falsehood commitments and betray from women. Extreme beautiful ladies are the enemies of their husbands because adultery and pseudo arrogance are found in them as their basic qualities. With such a beautiful lady, husband keeps over affection and lust hence forgets his duties for the parents and ritualistic obligations. He further says that the prostitutes who are of shy nature and the virtuous character ladies who are unabashed never survive for long because a prostitute can never earn her livings if she is of bashful nature and similarly a moral lady can never maintain her chastity if she is shameless by nature.

*Chanakya* says that it is far better to live a life of bachelor instead of marrying with a cruel lady of cunning nature. The only enemy of a lady of immoral character involved in debauchment is her husband who actually loves, provides living and gives moral advice to her.

एक एव पदार्थस्तु त्रिधा भवति वीक्षितः।
कुणपः कामिनी मांसं योगिभिः कामिभिः श्वभिः।।
प्रत्युराज्ञां बिना नारी उपोष्य व्रतचारिणी।
आयुष्यं हरते भर्तुः सा नारी नरकं व्रजेत।।

*Chanakya* says that for a single object there may be
different opinions. A saint considers the body of a beautiful
woman as a corpse and keeps no attraction towards her while
a sexually corrupt licentious man keeps deep infatuation with
her and for a dog, that beautiful woman is only be the source
of attraction when she dies and after funeral, her body part
become the food for him.

*Chanakya* says that a lady who keeps ritualistic fasting
or performs such obligations without the consent of her
husband deteriorates the life span of her husband and
endures the hell after death.

# *Vatsyayan Kamsutra*

*Kamsutra* of *Vatsyayan* is sufficient to describe the relations of men and women but the depiction done in this, pertaining to the temperament, conduct and persona of women is inadequate. Though it is clearly mentioned that the knowledge of *Kamsutra* is not for imprudent men but it is also found not to be meant for those who have true conscience or are ascetics by nature. Hence the knowledge of *Kamsutra* is fruitful for those virtuous men, who are trapped in the violent outburst of passionate feelings thereby getting bewildered because in qualities, such men lay in-between an amorous and an ascetic. A very clear depiction of the easy going tactics to allure other women and the different postures of sexual union is done in *Kamsutra* hence it is also capable to divert men of morals from their upright track. As per the opinion of scholars and highly erudite persons, the verses mentioned in *Kamsutra* does not provoke to men of high ethics to perform immoral acts instead they make them acquainted with the techniques by which they can protect their wives from committing illicit sexual transgression. If the study of *Kamsutra* is done scrupulously with the sagacity of distinguishing in-between the moral and immoral deeds in thought then it is found to be a very extraordinary treatise written on the sexual union of men and women. The definition of sexual pleasure given in this is as following:-

श्रोत्रत्वक्चक्षुतिह्वाघ्राणानामात्मसंयुक्तेन मनसाधिष्ठितानां
स्वेषु स्वेषु विषयेष्वानुकूल्यतः प्रवृत्तिः कामः ।।

The frequent attempt or effort done to achieve the sensation of sensual delight obtained through ear, skin, eyes, tongue and nose like melodious voice, excitement by touching, looking attractive sceneries or views from the eyes, delicious taste from tongue and enjoying the fragrance from nose, is termed as sexual or sensual association. The dexterity of the ladies in the art of sexual mating is appraised by the extent of their nimbleness in the sixty-four skills, which are the core of *Kamsutra*, and are as follows:-

गीतम् वाद्यम्, नृत्यम्, आलेख्यम्, विशेषकच्छेद्यम्,
तण्डुलकुसुमवलिविकारा:, पुष्पास्तरणम्, दशनवसनाङ्गराग:,
मणिभूमिकाकर्म, शयनरचनम्, उदकवाद्यम्, उदकाघात,
चित्राश्च योग:, माल्यग्रथनविकल्पा:, शेखरकापीडयोजनम्,
नेपथ्यप्रयोगा:, कर्णपत्रभङ्गा:, गन्धयुक्ति:, भूषणयोजनम्,
ऐन्द्रजाला:, कौचुमाराश्च योगा:, हस्तलाघवम्,
विचित्रशाकयूषभक्ष्यविकारक्रिया, पानकरसरागासवयोजनम्,
सूचीवानकर्माणि, सूत्रक्रीडा, वीणाड-मरूकवाद्यानि,
प्रहेलिका, प्रतिमाला, दुर्वाचकयोगा:, पुस्तकवाचनम्,
नाटकाख्यायिकादर्शनमृद्घ, काव्यसमस्यापूरणम्,
पट्टिकावानवेत्रविकल्पा:, तक्षकर्माणि, तक्षणम् वास्तुविद्या,
रूप्यपरीक्षा, धातुवाद:, मणिरागाकरज्ञानम्, वृक्षायुर्वेदयोगा:

मेषकुक्कुटलावकयुद्धविधि:, शुकसारिकाप्रलापनम्, उत्सादने
संवाहने केशमर्दने च कौशलम्, अक्षरमुष्टिकाकथनम्,
म्लेच्छितविकल्पा:, देशभाषा-विज्ञानम्, पुष्पशकटिका,
निमित्तज्ञानम्, यन्त्रमातृका, धारण-मातृका, सम्पाठ्यम्,
मानसी काव्य-क्रिया, अभिधानकाश:, छन्दो-ज्ञानम्, क्रियाकल्प:,
छलितकयोगा:, वस्त्रगोपनानि, द्यूतविशेष:, आकर्षक्रीडा,
बालक्रीडनकानि, वैनयिकीनाम्, वैजयिकीनाम्, व्यायामिकीनां
च विद्यानां ज्ञानम्, इति चतु: षष्टिरङ्गविद्या:
कामसूत्र-स्यावयविन्य: ।।

Art of singing, playing musical instruments, dancing, art
of painting, art of cutting in a decorative manner, making
painted decorations from the flour of rice and flowers on the
floors and walls, decorating an arched gateway with flowers,
attractive veneering on teeth, body and garments, decoration
of floors of buildings and courtyards with precious beads and
jewels, embellishment of bed, producing pleasant-to-hear
tunes by blowing in water or making melodious sound from
harmonica, producing sequential waves from the showers
while frolicking in water, knowledge of the treatment done by
charms or incantations and herbs, to arrange flowers in an
attractive way in a garland, decorating face and forehead by
jewelries, create attractiveness through the matching of
garments and jewelries, making jewelries from the origin of
pearl that is from shell, conch shell and ivory, dexterity in
making different fragranced liquid perfumes, making normal
jewelries attractive by fastening exclusive stones into it,

knowledge of games which bring hallucination and curiosity magic to create the impact of aphrodisiac or a romantic situation by making unnatural environment to appear as very natural, adroitness in fine work, preparation of different kinds of delicious foods, preparation of variety of drinks, knowledge of fine weaving or stitching, to engrave the pictures of animals, birds, buildings and synagogues on the cloths through handicraft work done by colored yarn or threads for decoration purpose, playing lute or *Vina* or other musical instruments producing harmonious sound, commonsense of solving puzzles and other abstruse queries, art of playing *Antyakashri*, a musical game in which each person has to sing a song with the last letter of the song sung by previous person, deep knowledge and ability to clearly pronounce the difficult words of Sanskrit language, art of announcing the verses of religious books properly in which some words are pronounced in high pitch and some in low pitch depending on the context of it, knowledge of ancient dramas and historical stories, skill of completing any incomplete verse of poetry, art of making useful and decorative items from cane, skill of the fine design work on gold, designing utensils, statues and toys from soil of clay, familiarity with the science of architecture, skill to inspect the worth of jewels, knowledge to produce different compounds by amalgamating different metals, identifying precious stones and familiarity with the method of their cutting and gilding, giving a beautiful shape to trees and creepers, ar to arranging the fighting of rams, cocks, grasshoppers and bulls, training parrots and mynahs to speak like human being, art of massaging over forehead, head and other body parts, knowledge of symbolic language, knowledge of allusive jargon, knowledge of the languages of different countries, making of exquisite chariots by flowers, ability to sense the incidents thereby forecasting about an auspicious omen or an ominous omen that is supposes to be happening in future, making of manually handled or automatic machines, knowledge of methods to increase the memory power, familiarity with the way to pronounce the religious verses and the art of making suitable verses from the abstruse typical words, knowledge of high flown language or expertise in morphology and phraseology, knowledge of poetic composition, master of deceitful act of magic to change own appearance and persona for amusement, art of looking short in long clothes and vice-versa, knowledge of gambling, art of throwing dice, art of hypnotism, familiarity with the games of kids, skilled in the codes of conduct, knowledge of economics and well familiarity with methods and proper way of physical exercise, gymnastics and practice of abstract meditation.

It is said that a *Ganika* did not lead a life of prostitute for the sake of earning money or sexual delight yet it is assumed that their actual origin and subsistence was active prostitution.

आभिरभ्युच्छिता वेश्या शीलरूपगुणान्विता ।
लभते गणिकाशब्दं स्थानं च जनसंसदि ।।

A beautiful prostitute, after being expertise in these sixty four arts of evoking sensual lust, becomes *Ganika*. Such *Ganikas* provide the knowledge of sex and techniques to other young prostitutes to get more skilled in the art of sex hence performing the responsibility of an educator, are considered to be worthy of social respect.

नरः कलासु कुशलो वाचालश्चाटुकारकः ।
असंस्तुतोऽपि नारीणां चित्तमाश्वेव विन्दति ।।

A man who does not possess any specific quality and belongs to deprived category can also fascinate a beautiful lady by his knack of vocalizations, toadying and performing sexual union in different postures. According to *kamsutra* ladies are of three types:-

तत्र नायिकास्तिस्रः कन्या पुनर्भूर्वेश्या च इति ।।

The three types of ladies are *Kanya*, *Punarbhu* and *Vaishya*. A virgin unmarried lady with virtuous qualities is termed as *Kanya*. A married or unmarried lady who keeps illicit sexual relations with other men for the sake of sexual pleasure only is said to be *Punarbhu*. A lady who earns her living by prostitution is said to be *Vaishya*.

Men who are passionate for sexual love are advised as to whom with they can keep such illicit relations. Though for

194

the men of morals and high ethics, keeping even a thought of such relations is prohibited.

अन्यतोऽपि बहुशो व्यवसितचारित्रा तस्यां वेश्यायामिव
गमनमुत्तमवर्णिन्यामपि न धर्मपीडां करिष्यति पुनर्भुरियम ।।
 - - - - - - - - - - - - - - - - - - - - - - - - - - -
अन्यपूर्वावरूद्धा नात्र शङ्कास्ति ।।

A lady who has become characterless due to regular illicit sexual relations or who has become the entity of attaining sexual enjoyment for men is not different from a prostitutes doesn't matter whether she belongs to a high or low dynasty. Thus, having sexual union with such lady is not amiss.

A man, who lacks conscience because of his passion of love, should keep moral conduct at the moment of stirring up of passion. In the following situations, a sexually corrupt man is not considered to be going against political wisdom even if he sexually intercourses with other lady:-

निरत्ययं वास्या गमनमर्थानुबद्धम् ।
अहं च निःसारत्वात्क्षीणवृत्त्युपायः ।
सोऽहमनेनोपायेन तद्धनमतिमहदकृच्छादधिगमिष्यामि ।।
मर्मज्ञा वा मयि दृढमभिकामा सा मामनिच्छन्तं दोषविख्यापनेन
दूषयिष्यति ।।
असद्वृतं वा दोषं श्रद्धेयं दुष्परिहारं मयि क्षेप्स्यति येन मे विनाशः
स्यात् ।।

If a husband of a particular lady financially betrays the other man, then in that case if that man is confident that through that lady he can take the revenge from her husband then he should not hesitate in making sexual relationship with that lady. It is not wrong to engage in sexual coalitions with other ladies if it can become a medium of getting the financial benefit. When a lady is familiar with the secrets of a man and threatens him to disclose those secrets if he does not make sexual relations with her, then to sexually intercourse with such a lady is not inappropriate. Such issues are frequently found in today's life. It is often found in present that if men do not fulfill the sexual and financial requirements of ladies, they deceptively accuse them for sexual pestering. According to Kamsutra:-

आयतिमन्तं वा वश्यं पतिं मत्तो विभिद्य द्विषतः संग्राहयिष्यति।।
स्वयं वा तैः सह संसृज्येत। मदवरोधानां वा दूषयिता
पतिरस्यास्तदस्याहमपि दारानेव दूषयन्प्रतिकरिष्यामि।।

If a man is sure that on ignoring the proposal of a lady for sexual course, she shall falsely blame him for sexual harassment then to keep sexual relations with such lady is not iniquitous. Again if a man does not fulfill the sexual desire of a strange or a familiar lady and that displeased lady tries to put false blames on that man in front of her husband and relatives so that they may become against to him, then due to the fear of the regard for public opinion, it is not iniquitous to have sexual relations with such lady.

The proper description of the type of ladies is given in context to their infatuation and physical association with men, in *Kamsutra*. If we consider such leading ladies as heroine or fiancée, then going beyond the morality or immorality, the following types of such ladies are described:-

एतैरेव कारणैर्महामात्रसंबद्धा राजसंबद्धा वा तत्रैकदेशचारिणी
काचिदन्या वा कार्यसम्पादिनी विधवा पन्चमीति चारायण: ।।
सैव प्रव्रजिता षष्टीति सुवर्णनाभ: ।।
गणिकाया दुहिता परिचारिका वानन्यपूर्वा सप्तमीति घोटकमुख: ।।
उत्क्रान्तबालभावा कुलयुवतिरूपचारान्यत्वादष्टमीति गोनर्दीय: ।।

Besides *Kanya*, *Punarbhu* and *Vaishya*, the fourth category of such ladies is another's wife. A widow who is related to the family of a king, minister, high dynasty or normal public is considered to be in the fifth category. Such ladies belonging to fifth category do not remarry instead they commit debauchment with other men. The sixth category of such ladies is who are living in solitude, being a wandering ascetic widow, seeking sexual pleasure because their husband has renounced the world and become ascetic after completing domestic phase or second stage of life. Young daughter of a *Ganika*, maid-servant or prostitute, who is enthusiastically ready for sexual activities, is considered in the seventh category. A girl, who just reaches to the stage of adolescence from the upbringing stage and gives the permission for sexual play on providing sensual temptations, belongs to eighth category. Such opinions are articulated by spiritual preceptors

197

*Charayan, Suvarnabh, Ghotakmukh* and *Gonardiya*. Thus or the basis of aforementioned opinions, it can be said that initia four types of such ladies are the source of rest of the fou types. It is said that men should not keep sexual relations with the following ladies as they are *Agamya* for them:-

अगम्यास्त्वेवैता:-कुष्ठिन्युन्मत्ता पतिता भिन्नरहस्या प्रकाशप्रार्थिनी गतप्राययौवनातिश्वेतातिकृष्णा दुर्गन्धा सम्बन्धिनी सखी प्रव्रजिता सम्बन्धिसखिश्रोत्रियराजदाराश्च ।।
दृष्टपन्चपुरूषा नागम्या काचिदस्तीति बाभ्रवीया: ।।
संबन्धिसखिश्रोत्रियराजदारवर्जमिति गोणिकापुत्र: ।।

Such thirteen kind of ladies with whom a man should not commit sexual intercourse are the one suffering from leprosy, mentally retarded, lapsed from the religion or who is outcaste, non-trustworthy or the one who cannot keep the secrets or of fraudulent nature, unabashed, old aged, of utter fair body color complexion, of very dark body color complexion, whose body stinks, very close relative to the chain of mother's or father's ancestors, very close friend o ladies whom with he possess high moral relations, a female renunciant and a lady belonging to the family of close relatives or friends or saints who keep knowledge of Vedas or of highe dynasty.

According to the opinion of saint *Brabhraviya*, if a lad of above thirteen categories has kept the illicit sexual relation with at least different five men other than her husband then to

198

commit sexual intercourse with her is not sinful because she is *Gamya* but according to saint *Gonikaputra*, a lady belonging to the family of a friend, a priests having the knowledge of Vedas and a high dynasty, should not be chosen for sexual course even if she has kept illicit relations with five men hence she is ever *Agamaya*.

The behavior and type of the lustful ladies and the actual demeanor shown by them are mentioned in *Kamsutra*. Though such kind of behavior is restricted for the ladies of high moral still they too are frequently found illustrating this type of performances.

यत्किंचिद् द्रष्टा विहसितं करोति।
तत्र कथामवस्थानार्थमनुबध्नाति।
बालस्याङ्कगस्यालिङ्गनं चुम्बनं च करोति।
परिचारिकायास्तिलकं च रचयति।
परिजनानवष्टभ्य तास्ताश्च लीला दर्शयति॥
बालक्रीडनकैर्बाला कलाभिर्यौवने स्थिता।
वत्सला चापि संग्राह्या विश्वास्यजनसंग्रहात्॥
प्रदोषे निशि तमसि च योषितो मन्दसाध्वसाः सुरतव्यवसायिन्यो
रागवत्यश्च भवन्ति।
न च पुरुषं प्रत्याचक्षते।
तस्मात्तत्कालं प्रयोजयितव्या इति प्रायोवादः॥
मन्दापदेशा गुणवत्यपि कन्या धनहीना कुलीनापि
समानैरयाच्यमाना मातापितृवियुक्ता वा ज्ञातिकुलवर्तिनी
वा प्राप्तयौवना पाणिग्रहणं स्वयमभीप्सेत्॥
पुष्पगन्धताम्बूलहस्ताया विजने विकाले च तदुपस्थानम्।

कला-कौशलप्रकाशने वा संवाहने शिरसः पीडने
चौचित्यदर्शनम् ।
प्रयोज्यस्य सात्त्वयुक्ताः कथायोगाः बालायामुपक्रमेषु
यथोक्तमाचरेत् ।।
न चैवान्तरापि पुरुषं स्वयमभियुञ्जीत । स्वयमभियोगिनी
हि युवतिः सौभाग्यं जहातीत्याचार्याः ।।
परिष्वक्ता च न विकृतिं भजेत् । श्लक्ष्णमाकारमजानतीव
प्रतिगृहीयात् ।
वदनग्रहणे बलात्कारः ।।

— — — — — — — — — — —

अभ्यर्थितापि नातिविवृता स्वयं स्यात् ।
अन्यत्रानिश्चयकालात् ।।
कन्याभियुज्यमाना तु यं मन्येताश्रयं सुखम् ।
अनुकूलं च वश्यं च तस्य कुर्यात्परिग्रहम् ।।
वरं वश्यो दरिद्रोऽपि निर्गुणोऽप्यात्मधारणः ।
गुणैर्युक्तोऽपि न त्वेवं बहुसाधारणः पतिः ।।
यदृच्छयाभियुक्तो यो दम्भद्यूताधिकोऽपि वा ।
सपत्नीकश्च सापत्यो न स संयोगमर्हति ।।

Ladies, who are in love, pass gentle and modest smile
while looking at their lovers. They try to fascinate their lover by
mellifluously talking to others in front of him. They embrace
and love a kid to draw the attention of their lovers and to
sexually provoke them, when they are not able to control over
their own obsession for love. Thus the moment they are
sexually impassioned by the presence of suitable lover, they
give silent indication of their sexual feeling by lifting a small
child in arms, kissing him and stroking his hair with caress.

Female lovers are of three types on the basis of their age group and sexual acquaintance. Girls who act childish and are found playing games of children are said to be *Bala*, young ladies who have the ignorance as well as the awareness of sexual knowledge or who neither are fully known nor unknown to sensual pleasure, keeping passion for lust towards men are said to be *Taruni* and the ladies who are theoretically as well as practically clued-up about sexual relations are known as *Prauda*. The ladies become passionate for love for their lovers during evening and night, in a secluded spot. Thus, in this situation, if they are proposed by a man for sexual coalition, they become overwhelmed and give their consent.

If any girl possesses virtuous and appreciating qualities but associated to an inferior dynasty or is orphan or is financially unfortunate or belongs to a family in destitution, then she herself should try for her marriage instead of waiting for her elders to do so.

A lustful lady should try to attract the suitable man or should allure him for sexual intercourse by the use of sixty four arts of *Kamsutra*, in an isolated spot or in the night or when he is in sorrow because of the demise of some of his close relative as in aforesaid three situations, the little effort of her make the man sentimental to express his feelings. Ladies should try to seduce their suitable men by revealing their body

parts but even in the situation of being impatient because o
stirring up of passion, they should neither request nor take
initiative to start sexual play, instead they should preser
themselves in such an alluring way that men beseech them fo
the same thing. Such lustful ladies should control themselve
while their lover touches, embraces and kisses them at the
moment of love-making. Such ladies should never disclose
their previous experiences and proficiency in the art of making
sex hence should pretend as an innocent and unaware of the
art of sex or sexual knowledge. If they act as a novice thereby
hiding their adroitness in making sexual course, their husband
or lovers may never be able to predict about their previou
sexual relations with other men. This is the very commor
behavior shown by morally corrupt ladies because almost o
them even after being involved in illicit sexual relations in past
express shyness in the first night, in front of their lovers o
husband and behave in such a peculiar way of hesitation
thereby pretending to be frightened of a touch as if they wi
lose their virginity.

A lady with practical wisdom, if loves a man with the
purpose of marriage then she should not get easily ready to
keep sexual relations with him and should not reveal her body
parts being fully stripped on his request before marriage
because in future he may become doubtful of her character
and shall not marry her. If a lady is orphan or her parents are
not capable or are unwilling to make her marry then she

should herself select a worthy man for marriage. A lady should prefer a well character man for marriage, able to earn living and having sense of prudence, doesn't matter if he belongs to a financially deprived family, instead of marrying a wealthy and handsome looking man involved in debauchment. Ladies have been directed not to marry with a man who under protest keeps sexual relations with them before marriage or is shrewd by nature or involved in professional gambling or is already married and possess kids. It is instructed to the virtuous character and husband devotee ladies to maintain the physical as well as mental purity and being of high ethics is their only religion.

भिक्षुकीश्रमणाक्षपणा कुलटाकुहकेक्षणि कामूलकारिकाभिर्न
संसृज्येत ।।
अतिव्ययमसव्ययं वा कुर्वाणं रहसि बोधयेत् ।।
साधिक्षेपवचनं त्वेनं मित्रजनमध्यस्थमेकाकिनं वाप्युपालभेत ।
न च मूलकारिका स्यात् ।।
नद्व्रतोऽन्यदप्रत्ययकारणमस्तीति गोनर्दीयः ।।
दुर्व्याहृतं दुर्निरीक्षितमन्वतो मन्त्रणं द्वारदेशावस्थानं निरीक्षणं
वा निष्कुटेषु मन्त्रणं विविक्तेषु चिरमवस्थानमिति वर्जयेत् ।।
श्वश्रूश्वशुरपरिचर्या तत्पारतन्त्र्यमनुत्त रवादिता
परिमिताप्रचण्डालापकरणमनुच्चैर्हासः तत्प्रियाप्रियेषु
स्वप्रियाप्रियेष्विव वृत्तिः ।।
नायकस्यानिवेद्य न कस्मैचिद्दानम् ।।

A husband devotee lady should not accompany herself with the ladies who beg to earn their living being ascetic but in fact are shrewd, female renunciants who blames the married life, ladies involved in dancing and singing publicly to earn fo living, adulteress, and female witch magician or ladies involved in harming others by the help of black magic. If a husband spends money unnecessary on the wife to gratify he or in worthless deeds then the wife should considerately advise him not to do so. If the husband is involved in any type of immoral activity then it is the obligation of wife to guide him courteously when he is alone with her. A lady should always behave properly with her husband and should never disclose the blunders of her husband in front of others. Again if the husband is diverted from the righteous track then wife should guide him in a proper way in spite of taking the help of witch doctors to change his nature by the help of black magic Ladies who take the help of witch doctors to control their husbands or to change the thoughts of them through the black magic are never succeeded in their malicious attempts and troubles the life of their husbands. Such ladies never achieve the trust and love of their husband. Every married lady should obey and respect her husband's parents and other elder blood relatives. To converse in high pitch, amusing stridently and retorting in an indecent behavior is prohibited for the ladies in front of in-laws elder to her. A married lady should help her brothers, parents or other relatives of before marriage or after marriage only on the consent of her husband. Married lady should not financially help any one unless her husband gives permission for that. Regarding the marriage of a man with more than one ladies or polygamy, it is said that:-

जाड्यदौःशील्यदौर्भाग्येभ्यः प्रजानुत्पत्तेराभीक्ष्ण्येन
दारिकोत्पत्तेर्नायकचापलाद्वा सपत्न्यधिवेदनम् ।।

A man commits more than one marriage in following conditions: having lack of conscience, being characterless, lack of progeny, having daughters but no son and the tendency to commit adultery. In the above mentioned reasons, being characterless and involvement in debauchment or illicit sexual relations appears to be complementary to each other but yet not same. The tendency of debauchery can be restrained while if the overall character is polluted, nothing can be done. Beside the above minor reasons there are few major reasons responsible for the remarriage done by a man either by breaking of first marriage or keeping more than one wife at a time and these foremost causes are the previous wife's being of ill character, inhuman nature, mental retarded, sexually impotent or unnecessary denying the request of husband done for the love making, rude behavior and keeping active skepticism towards him.

यतस्तु स्वेच्छया पुनरपि निष्क्रमणं निर्गुणोऽयमिति तदान्यं
काङ्क्षेदिति बाभ्रवीयाः ।।
सौख्यार्थिनी सा किलान्यं पुनर्विन्देत ।।
गुणेषु सोपभोगेषु सुखसाकल्यं तस्मात्ततो विशेष इति गोनर्दीयः ।।

A lady who is unsatisfied mentally and physically from her husband becomes emotionally involved with other man and further keeps illicit sexual relations with him. Such mental discontent may be because of aggressive nature of husband and quarrelling nature of the wife. Physical dissatisfaction occurs because of the inadequate or appropriate sexual feelings in husband while unrestrained and unlimited sexual desires of wife. Such a lady who is not sexually satisfied with her husband, on stirring up of passion, involves herself into making illicit sexual relationship and called as *Punarbhu*.

In fact, the sensual love and satisfaction for which she pursues here and there has no limit and does not exist. Thus for seeking sexual satisfaction, she involves herself into illicit relations with numerous people and includes herself in the category of Prostitutes. The ten symptoms of the factual affection produced in a man for a lady and the propensities of women are clearly illustrated as:-

चक्षुःप्रीतिर्मनासङ्गः संकल्पोत्पत्तिनिद्राच्छेदस्तनुता विषयेभ्यो
व्यावृत्तिर्लज्जाप्रणाश उन्मादो मूर्च्छा मरणमिति तेषां लिङ्गानि।।
व्यभिचारादाकृतिलक्षणयोगानामिङ्गिताकाराभ्यामेव प्रवृत्तिर्बोद्धव्या
योषित इति वात्स्यायनः।।
न स्त्री धर्ममधर्मं चापेक्षते कामयत एव। कार्यापिक्षया तु
नाभियुङ्क्ते।।

स्वभावाच्च पुरुषेणाभियुज्यमाना चिकीर्षन्त्यपि व्यावर्तते।।

पुनः पुनरभियुक्ता सिद्धयति।।
निष्कारणमभियुङ्क्ते। अभियुज्यापि पुनर्नाभियुङ्क्ते।
सिद्धायां च माध्यस्थयं गच्छति।।
सुलभामवमन्यते। दुर्लभामाकाङ्क्षत इति प्रायोवादः।

Love is seen in the eyes of an overwhelmed man being overflowed of tears while he looks at his beloved or gets away from her, mind and heart captivated by his lover's romantic thoughts, performing special efforts to get the proximity of her, loss of somnolence due to her reminiscence, not taking care of own health and thereby becomes lean, being unaffected from other beautiful ladies and getting averse to them, giving up the bashfulness thereby not caring for the public opinion, performing senseless and ridiculous acts like an absurd person and even embrace the death by committing suicide. According to *Vatsyayan*, a woman's body shape, behavior and the birth marks or symbols marked on her body by birth, are helpful to know about her character.

A lady does not think about the religion, honor of the family and moral-immoral while making love with fiancé or with any man in order to satisfy her sexual need but if it is found by her that she can be blamed by the society or family members, she quits the relationship by falsely blaming on the sex partner for seducing her. If a lady finds her future insecure with her fiancé who is unemployed or lacking self dependency or unable to earn to gratify her by precious gifts then she ends the love-affair. On the further attempts of a man to request that lady, if she agrees then they continue such relationship but again on finding that he is still not able to provide him security and wealth, she lands up ending the relationship. When a relationship is ended by a lady because o aforementioned reasons then if that clever licentious love tries on gratifying her, he can get the triumph by achieving he for sexual pleasure. When a lady keeps the physical relatior with a man, she wants to continue over it thereby marrying t that fiancé but that man as a lover may become reluctant ir order to accept her as his wife. A lady who readily permits he lover for making sexual intercourse, is not easily accepted by him as his wife because a thought always infuriates such mar that his fiancée would have perpetrated sexual coalition witl other men in past as she was easy to lay. According t Kamsutra, the ladies who keep the desire of keeping sexua relations with other men or who attracts lustful men or who are easily available for sexual coalition have the following properties and behavior:-

अयत्नसाध्या योषितस्त्विमाः-अभियोगमात्रसाध्याः ।
द्वारदेशाव-स्थायिनी । प्रासादाद्राजमार्गावलोकिनी ।
तरुणप्रातिवेश्यगृहे गोष्ठीयोजिनी ।
सततप्रेक्षिणी । प्रेक्षिता पार्श्वविलोकिनी ।
निष्कारणं सपत्न्याधिविन्ना ।
भर्तृद्वेषिणी विद्विष्टा च । परिहारहीना । निरपत्या ॥

ज्ञातिकुलनित्या। विपन्नापत्या। गोष्ठीयोजिनी।
प्रीतियोजिनी। कुशीलवभार्या। मृतपतिका बाला।
दरिद्रा बहूपभोगा। ज्येष्ठभार्या बहुदेवरका।
बहुमानिनी न्यूनभर्तृका।
कौशलाभिमानिनी भर्तुर्मौख्येणो-द्विग्ना।
अविशेषतया लोभेन।।
कन्याकाले यत्नेन वारिता कथंचिदलब्धाभियुक्ता च सा
तदानीम्। समानबुद्धिशीलमेधाप्रतिपत्तिसात्म्या।
प्रकृत्या पक्षपातिनी। अनपराधे विमानिता।
तुल्यरूपाभिश्चाधः कृता। प्रोषितपतिकेति।
ईर्ष्यालुपूति-चोक्षक्तीवदीर्घसूत्र-
कापुरुषकुब्जवामनविरूपमणिकारग्राम्य दुर्गन्धिरोगिवृद्ध-
भार्याश्चेति। अनभियुक्ताप्याकारयति। विविक्ते
चात्मानं दर्शयति। सर्वेष्वथुगद्गदं वदति।
स्विन्नकरचरणाङ्गुलिः स्विन्नमुखी च भवति।
शिरःपीडने संवाहने चोर्चोरात्मानं नायके
नियोजयति।।

The lady who continuously stands on the door and
looks out at the passage, the one who stands on the terrace
and exchanges the glances of the neighbor's house or on
road with curious intentions, who does continuous
unnecessary conversation with the known or unknown youth,
keeps an eye on the visitors of neighbor's house, looks with a
lustful sidelong glance to the youths who admire her, always
shows herself depressed because of being skeptical about
extra-marital affairs of the husband even when such affairs
are not in existence, is always sexually unsatisfied because of
her acute obsession for love hence perpetually keeps

209

antagonism with the husband unnecessarily, is abhorred by the husband because of being of vindictive conduct and quarrelling disposition, possesses the tendency of perpetrating debauchment, is barren, stays at father's residence for a long time thereby leaving husband without any reason and involved in resuscitating the pre marriage love affairs, is *Mratvatsa* or gives birth to dead children or whose children die after birth, never accepts the difference between right and wrong person hence keeps close affinity with any category's lady, commits harlotry under the shade of her profession of singing or dancing, is the widow of very young age or child widow, is a destitute possessing very greedy nature hence eager to earn money by any means, keeps the same closeness with the friends of her husband as with her husband's brother, is extreme fascinated by her own beauty hence feels inferiority complex while being with the husband and thus treats her husband despairingly, is of arrogant nature, whose husband is indolent hence possesses lack of proper earnings, is weary of her husband while sexually fascinated by other men, the one who does not get the desired husband or a husband of her own imagination, is equal or more knowledgeable in comparison to her husband or earns living of her by herself thereby not depending on husband's income, is fascinated with some specific man, is unnecessarily scolded by husband or in-laws, lives away from her husband, is married to a unhygienic man, is puzzled because of the extreme jealous nature of her husband, is married to a man of mean mentality, is unnecessarily physically tortured by husband, is married to a sexually impotent person or coward, is married with an ugly looking man or a man involved in illicit extramarital sexual relations, is married to a man suffering from incurable diseases and is married to an overage man in comparison to herself gets ready for the illicit sexual relations on little effort.

Again it is said about the easy-going or easy to get ladies that who are extrovert thereby intermingles with the strange men also, who without any introduction show their lust by expressions, who are eager to reveal their body to specific man in an isolated place, who loudly express their stirring up of passion during the conversation with men, who pretends unfailing trust on other men by gently speaking, who start to sweat while talking to men and the drops of sweat are generally seen on feet, palms and face of them and who do not object and hesitate on touching by a man can be seduced easily for making love. The following description is done in context of unnatural sexual relations:-

नान्तः पुराणां रक्षणयोगात्पुरुषसंदर्शनं विद्यते
पत्युश्चैकत्वादनेकसाधारणत्वाच्चातृप्तिः ।
तस्मात्तानि प्रयोगत एवं परस्परं रञ्जयेयुः ॥
धात्रेयिकां सखीं दासीं व पुरुषवदलंकृत्याकृतिसंयुक्तैः
कन्दमूलफलावयवैरपद्रव्यैर्वात्माभिप्रायं निवर्तयेयुः ॥

स्त्रीयोगेणैव पुरुषाणामप्यलब्धवृत्तीनां वियोनिषुविजातिषु
स्त्रीप्रतिमासु केवलोपमर्दनाच्चाभिप्राय निवृत्तिर्व्याख्याता।।

The queens residing in the women's quarters in a palace are usually sexually unsatisfied because of a single king as their husband hence if they find it impossible to get the sexual pleasure from other men through illicit sexual relations they take the help of unnatural and artificial ways to calm down their passion of lust. They ask the daughters of wet nurse, foster-mother or concubines to wear the dress of male like a man and lie down over them thereby making them sexually excited by kissing and massaging the breasts. They order to young lady servant to insert the vegetables or fruit as an artificial penis in their vagina so as to create sexual sensation through rubbing. Men also in the absence of ladies try to sexually satisfy themselves by doing the masturbation or committing unnatural sexual mating with a statue of woman contrived *Yoni* or artificial vagina and female animals like a mare or bitch.

There is a typical description of the qualities tendencies, duties, and activities of a prostitute done in the *Kamsutra*. The description done of the behavior of the prostitutes in *Kamsutra* is found somewhere to be dissimilar from the attitude of the prostitutes found in the present atmosphere

वेश्यानां पुरुषाधिगमे रतिर्वृत्तिश्च सर्गात्।।

---

रतितः प्रवर्तनं स्वाभाविकं कृत्रिममर्थार्थम्।।

---

न चानुपायेनार्थान् साधयेदायतिसंरक्षणार्थम्।।
ते त्वारक्षकपुरुषा धर्माधिकरणस्था दैवज्ञा विक्रान्ताः शूराः
समानविद्याः कलाग्राहिणः
पीठमर्दविटविदूषकमालाकारगान्धिकशौण्डिकरज.
कनापितभिक्षुकास्ते च ते च कार्ययोगात्।।
क्षयी रोगी कृमिशकृद्वायसास्यः प्रियकलत्रः परुषवाक्कदर्यो
निर्घृणो गुरुजनपरित्यक्तः स्तेनो दम्भशीलो मूलकर्मणि
प्रसक्तो मानापमानयोरनपेक्षी द्वेष्यैरप्यर्थहार्यो विलज्ज
इत्यगम्याः।।
रागो भयमर्थः संघर्षो वैरनिर्यातनं जिज्ञासा पक्षः खेदो धर्मो
यशोऽनुकम्पा सुहृद्वाक्यं हीः प्रियासादृश्यं धन्यता रागापनयः
साजात्यं साहवेश्यं सातत्यमायतिश्च गमनकारणानि
भवन्तीत्याचार्याः।।
रागापनयः साजात्यं साहवेश्यं सातत्यमायतिश्च
गमनकारणानि भवन्तीत्याचार्याः।।
अर्थोऽनर्थप्रतीघातः प्रीतिश्चेति वात्स्यायनः।।

---

चतुः षष्ट्यां शिष्यत्वम्।।

---

तदुपदिष्टानां च योगानामाभीक्ष्ण्येनानुयोगः।।
सूक्ष्मत्वादतिलोभाच्च प्रकृत्याज्ञानतस्तथा। कामलक्ष्म तु
दुर्ज्ञानं स्त्रीणां तन्वितैरपि।।
कामयन्ते विरज्यन्ते रन्ज्यन्ति त्यजन्ति च।
कर्षयन्त्योऽपि सर्वार्थाञ्ज्ञायन्ते नैव योषितः।।
देशं कालं स्थितिमात्मनो गुणान्सौभाग्यं चान्याभ्यो।
न्यूनातिरिक्तां चावेक्ष्य रजन्यामर्थं स्थापयेत्।।

प्रसन्ना ये प्रयच्छन्ति स्वल्पेऽप्यगणितं वसु ।
स्थूललक्षान्महोत्साहांस्तानगछेत्वैरपि व्ययैः ॥

संभूय च विटाः परिगृह्णन्त्येकामसौ गोष्ठीपरिग्रहः ॥

सा तेषामितस्ततः संसृज्यमाना प्रत्येकं संघर्षादर्थं निर्वर्तयेत् ॥
कुम्भदासी परिचारिका कुलटा स्वैरिणी नटी शिल्पकारिका
प्रकाशविनष्टा रूपाजीवा गणिका चेति वेश्याविशेषाः ॥
सन्ति रागपरा नार्यः सन्ति चार्थपरा अपि । प्राक्तत्र वर्णितो
रागो वेश्यायोगाश्च वैशिके ॥

Prostitutes are money-minded and the basic tendency found in them is always being ready for sexual intercourse. They have a natural fascination towards sex and desire for money is there simulated propensity. But in today's scenario the proclivity in prostitutes towards money is found to be inborn. A prostitute, in order to maintain her dignity, should ask for money from customer after providing him sexual pleasure. The duty of the helpers of the prostitute is to provide her social and administrative protection in emergency. Following people can be helpful to such prostitutes:– defender of prostitute or a pimp, high authority person involved in illicit sexual relations, advocate, forecaster, brave man, courageous man, artist, acrobat, jester, gardener, maker or seller of perfumes, wine seller, washerman, barber and vagabond.

A prostitute should not sexually intercourse with a man having specific physical symptoms, nature and status described below. She should not keep relations with a man

214

who is suffering from tuberculosis, leprosy, diseases which spread easily or a contagious disease, whose mouth stinks, who is wife devotee, is of quarrelsome nature, is a deserter, is of vindictive temperament, is debarred by parents, is a burglar, is a man with supercilious tendency, keeps the knowledge of black magic to harm others, having no self-respect, is a traitor and one who is unabashed by nature.

The main reasons behind sexual attachment are the infatuation of a man and a woman towards each other, fear, financial gain, struggle or competition, revenge, favoritism, dejection, objective of religious gain or inclination towards spiritual knowledge, achievement of fame, look of favor, sweet talks, over shyness, resemblance in thoughts, malicious intentions or antagonism, shared community and propinquity with each other. Such conditions if sustain for long, be the cause of obvious sexual attachment between a man and woman.

According to *Vatsyayan*, there are three basic reasons behind sexual coalition and these are covetousness for fiscal benefit, regard for public opinion or fear of public menace and affection. A prostitute should not prove herself proficient in the art of sexual intercourse and should not take initiatives by removing her cloths instead she should follow the instructions given by man or her customer thereby proving herself a novice in the sexual knowledge. It is impossible for a man to be familiar with the nature and tendencies of voracious prostitutes as they adopt every possible way to snatch away money and other precious items of their male customers. Prostitutes are attracted towards men only till the time they can fetch money from them.

A prostitute should fix her rate thereby appraise herself according to financial status or paying capacity of the people of the country she is living, own current status, her age and level of physical beauty, dexterity in sexual activities, popularity in customers and the charges of other contemporary prostitutes. They should not hesitate in spending their money as bait in order to give fodder to allure rich stupid profligate men to acquire money from them in future.

The method by which licentious and undiscriminating men do the mass sexual intercourse with a single prostitute is said to be *Goshthi Parigraha*, a kind of orgy. In such circumstances, the prostitute should take money from all men by emotionally or by argument.

Prostitutes are of nine types:- *Kumbhdasi, Paricharika Kulta, Swarini, Nati, Shilpkarika, Prakashvinashta, Rupjiva* and *Ganika*. This classification is in the increasing order of their financial level and sexual skills. Hence *Ganika* is the most skilled and renowned while *Kumbhdasi* is the one with least sexual appealing qualities. Many prostitutes sexually intercourse with their specific man due to an attraction or love attachment and then takes the financial help from him. Such a prostitute who keeps illicit relations with a single man and cared by him as his wife is known as *Rupjiva* or concubine. It is said in the context of the selection of a girl for marriage that:-

सवर्णायामनन्यपूर्वायां शास्त्रतोऽधिगतायां धर्मोऽर्थः पुत्राः सम्बन्धः
पक्षवृद्धिरनुपस्कृता रतिश्चच ।।
तस्मात्कन्यामभिजनोपेतां मातापितृमतीं त्रिवर्षात्रिभृति न्यूनवयसं
श्लाघ्याचारे धनवति पक्षवति कुले सम्बन्धिप्रिये सम्बन्धिभिराकुले
प्रसूतां प्रभूतमातृपितृपक्षां
रूपशीललक्षणसंपन्नामन्यूनाधिकाविनष्टदन्तनखकर्णकेशाक्षि-
स्तनीमरोगिप्रकृतिशरीरां तथाविध एव श्रुत्वाऽऽशीलयेत् ।।
सुप्तां रूदतीं निष्क्रान्तां वरणे परिवर्जयेत् ।।
अप्रशस्तनामधेयां च गुप्तां दत्तां घोनां पृषतामृषभां विनतां
विकटां विमुण्डां शुचिदूषितां सांकरिकीं राकां फलिनीं मित्रां
स्वनुजां वर्षकरीं च वर्जयेत् ।।
देशप्रवृत्तिसात्म्याद्धा ब्राह्मप्राजापत्यार्षदैवानामन्यतमेन विवाहेन
शास्त्रतः परिणयेत् । इति वरण विधानम् ।।
समस्याद्याः सहक्रीडा विवाहाः सङ्गतानि च ।
समानैरेव कार्याणि नोत्तमैर्नापि वाधमैः ।।

If a man marries with proper rituals to a virgin girl belonging to his community and caste then the couple experiences augmentation in mutual affection, progeny, wealth and moral deeds.

A man with conscience should marry a girl who possesses the following qualities:- The one who is of upright conduct, who is not orphan, younger than the man, belongs to respected family, whose progeny chain is known and who is beautiful looking with balanced body parts. Here orphan girl does not mean to a girl with no parents or family members or a girl in destitute. In fact here orphan indicates to a girl with lack of restraint and free from the honor of the family thereby involved in sexual debauchery. One should also not marry to a girl living in his society whose elders and parents are dead or not known because may be her demised parents would have a blood relation to his parents.

One should not marry with a lady who loves to sleep or live in idleness, whimpers unnecessary, is of quarrelsome nature and does not feel coyness in behaving awkwardly with men thereby leaving constraint and conventionality behind. A lady who is of distorted awful name, who spitefully conceals her identity, whose betroth was done but could not marry because of the mistakes of herself or her hypocrite family members, who has brown hair, suffers from leprosy or some incurable disease, possesses extraordinarily heavy buttocks, whose nape of the neck is over bent, having manly body figure, with very less hair on the head, involved in debauchment, deaf and dumb, familiar from the childhood, mentally or physically retarded, always sick thus of very thin body or the one who possesses name of the star, river or tree and the one whose name ends with "l" or "r" in it's pronunciation in Hindi language.

218

After the betrothal the marriage should be done either by *Braham*, *Prajapatya*, *Aarsh* or *Dev* marriages as per rituals. The three activities as playing games or having competition, searching life partner for marriage and friendship should be done with the people having same financial, social and moral status. According to *Kamasutra*, the daily routine of life after marriage should be as following:-

संगतयोस्त्रिरात्रमध शय्या ब्रह्मचर्यं क्षारलवणर्जमाहारस्तथा सप्ताहं
सतूर्यमङ्गलस्त्रानं प्रसाधनं सहभोजनं च प्रेक्षा सम्बन्धिनां च
पूजनम् । पूर्वं कायेण चोपक्रमेत् । विष हत्वात् ।।
सर्वा एव हि कन्याः पुरुषेण प्रयुज्यमानं वचनं विषहन्ते ।
न तु लघुमिश्रामपि वाचं वदन्ति । इति घोटकमुखः ।।
द्वितीयस्यां तृतीयस्यां च रात्रौ किंचिदधिकं विस्त्रम्भितां हस्तेन
योजयेत् ।। रशनावियोजनं नीवीविस्त्रंसनं
वसनपरिवर्तनमूरूमूलसंवाहनं च । एते चास्यान्यापदेशाः ।
युक्तयन्त्रां रन्जयेत् । न त्वकाले व्रतखण्डनम् ।।
युक्त्यापि तु यतः प्रसरमुपलभेतेनैवानु प्रविशेत् ।।
नात्यन्तमानुलोम्येन न चातिप्रातिलोम्यतः ।
सिद्धिं गच्छति कन्यासु तस्मान्मध्येन साधयेत् ।।

Married couple should sleep on floor for the first three nights and should neither perform the complete sexual intercourse nor should let their seminal fluid discharge. They should involve themselves in limited sexual activities. They should not eat spicy food and should take regular bath and wear decorated clothing. The couple should take meal with other family members and pay the respect to the elders every morning by touching their feet.

219

During the first night, husband should not make her wife feel uncomfortable and should only touch her upper body parts as her breast and should not even touch her lower body or below the navel. It is often found that newly married ladies even after being garrulous and iniquitous, silently listen to the husband's statements and do not retaliate or gossip insensibly in the very early days after marriage. Again a husband should try to make feel his wife comfortable in first night and during the second and third night he should touch and kiss her navel portion and thighs. In the forthcoming night, he should remove her ornamental belt of waist and thereby should make her *Sari* loose and take away her undergarments making her entirely stripped. He should touch the joints of her thighs or the vaginal lips in order to make her feel contented. A husband should not involve himself into complete intercourse without touching or sexually exciting her body. Thus when the wife entrust her self to husband illustrating her unspoken acquiescence and gets stress-free, he should insert his penis in her *Yoni* or vagina.

A husband should not excessively down his image or bow in front of his wife to make her easy and comfortable because wife may scold him in future for his such un-mannish behaviour. It is often found that wives consider husbands to be imprudent and themselves to be elegant if husbands bow before them desiring the love of them and making them feel relaxed.

सर्व सर्वत्र। रागस्यानपेक्षितत्वात् इति वात्स्यायनः।।
ललाटालक-कपोल-नयन वक्षः स्तनोष्ठान्तर्मुखेषु चुम्बनम्।।
ऊरुसंधिबाहुनाभिमूलयोर्लाटानाम्।।

According to *Vatsyayan*, there is no binding on the duration and method of sexual coalition. There is no specific rule for a lustful couple regarding the time when sexual intercourse should be done, for how long it should continue, what should be the process or posture of mating. Forehead, hair, cheeks, eyes, breasts, lips, the inner part of the mouth and tongue are the parts of lady's body appropriate for kissing. Though some men even prefer to kiss the lips of *Yoni* or vagina, joints of thighs, joints of arms or shoulders and lower belly part. The following is said in context of satisfaction and pleasure attained by women during sexual coalition:-

कथमेतदुपलभ्यत इति चेत्पुरुषो हि रतिमधिगम्य
स्वेच्छया विरमति, न स्त्रियमपेक्षेत, न त्वेवं स्त्रीत्यौद्दालकिः
सातत्याद्युवतिरारम्भाद्यत्रभृति भावमधिगच्छति। पुरुषः
पुनरन्त एव। एतदुपपन्नतरम्। नह्यसत्यां भावप्राप्तौ
गर्भसम्भव इति बाभ्रवीयाः।।

According to sage *Audhalik*, whether a lady attains the same pleasure and satisfaction like man during sexual intercourse or not, could be understood in the following way. After the sexual coalition or the discharge of seminal fluid, man becomes relaxed and gets averted from lady while such looseness, discharge and aversion is not seen in ladies. According to unity of opinion of the followers of educator

*Babhraviya*, man feels ultimate sexual pleasure at the time of seminal discharge and after that moment, the feeling of pleasure diminishes and he becomes tired. A lady experiences the sexual pleasure and satisfaction from the initial touching by man, kissing, embracing, kneading her breasts and mating. The outcome of the extreme pleasure experienced by a lady at the time of sexual intercourse is pregnancy.

विरूतानि चाष्टौ ।।
हिंकारस्तनितकूजितरुदितसूत्कृतफूत्कृतानि ।।
अम्बार्थाः शब्दा वारणार्था मोक्षणार्थाश्चालमर्थास्ते ते चार्थयोगात् ।।
रतान्ते च श्वसितरुदिते ।।
वेणोरिव स्फुटतः शब्दानुकरणं दूत्कृतम् ।।
अप्सु बदरस्येव निपततः फूत्कृतम् ।।

A lady who experiences the pleasure or satisfaction during sexual mating produces eight kinds of sound. The sound resembles the pronunciation of "Hi-Hi", a solemn resonating sound as "HH", uttering a shrill cry as a peacock, like taking deep breath or wailing or murmuring, sound resembling the pronunciation of "Su-Su", phrases indicating pain, request to stop pushes by expressing herself to be sexually satisfied and expressing the pain felt if partner still continues mating. Here wailing or murmuring indicates the puffing of woman at the finishing of sexual course. The sound produced at the time of sexual intercourse resembling like the pronunciation of "chat-chat" or "fuch-fuch" which is similar to the sound produced while tearing the bamboo pole is called *Dootkrat*. If the sound resembling like the pronunciation of "dub" is produced similar to the sound produced when a small plum like fruit of jujube tree falls in the water is called *Phutkrat*. The sound of *Dootkrat* is produced when whole of the penis is frequently inserted and put out from the vagina in a very fast way while the sound of *Phutkrat* is produced when only the edge or the upper part of the penis is put in and out of vagina in a fast manner.

शशो वृषोऽश्वइति लिङ्गतो नायकविशेषाः। नायिका
पुनर्मृगी वडवा हस्तिनी चेति।।

तत्र सदृशसंप्रयोगे समरतानि त्रीणि।।
यस्य संप्रयोगकाले प्रीतिरुदासीना वीर्यमल्पं क्षतानि च न सहते
स मन्दवेगः।।
तद्विपर्ययौ मध्यमचण्डवेगौ भवतः। तथा नायिकापि।।

तद्वत्कालतोऽपि शीघ्रमध्यचिरकाला नायकाः।।
प्रथमरते चण्डवेगता शीघ्रकालता च पुरुषस्य,
तद्विपरीतमुत्तरेषु। योषितः पुनरेतदेव विपरीतम्।
आ धातुक्षयात्।।

On the basis of the size or dimensions of the penis and depth of the vagina, men-women are divided in three parts:-

*Sash* man :- Man like a rabbit :- Penis of small dimension

*Rishabh* man :- Man like a bull :- Penis of medium dimension

*Ashwa* man :- Man like a horse :- Penis of large dimension

*Mrigi* lady :- Woman like a deer :- Yoni or vagina of less depth

*Ashwai* lady :- Woman like a mare :- Yoni or vagina of medium depth

*Hastani* lady :- Woman like a female horse :- Yoni of higher depth

In this way the sexual coalition of *Sash* man with *Mrig* lady, *Rishabh* man with *Ashwai* lady and *Ashwa* man with *Hastani* lady is considered to be a proper matching for sexual mating hence termed as *Sum Rati*. Rest of the six possible combinations of man and woman are sexually not fit hence called *Wisham Rati* or unequal levels of sex. Again on the basis of level of sexual attachment and extent of cooperation with which man-woman participate in the sexual mating, they are divided in to three types:-

Low speedy man :- Man with low passion for sex or a passionless :- The one who possesses low sexual excitement and early discharge of seminal fluid in less quantity during mating hence unable to satisfy lady.

Medium speedy man :- Man with medium leveled passion for love making.

High speedy man :- Man with extreme passion for love making :- The one who performs sexual mating with his whole sole temperament and fully satisfies a lady.

Low speedy lady :- Lady with low passion for sex or aversion to sex or a passionless :- The one who seldom gets ready for sexual mating and mostly be neutral towards sexual pleasure hence never cooperates with man during the mating.

Medium speedy lady :- Lady who cares of the sexual desire of the husband and performs sexual intercourse as a formality.

High speedy lady :- A lustful lady fully cooperating with husband in sexual mating.

The combination of above three types of men and three types of ladies make nine combinations of couple. On the basis of the duration of the process of sexual mating, men-women again are divided in three types. These three types are as men-women whose seminal fluid discharges very easily, who involve themselves in a sexual activity for a normal duration and whose seminal fluid discharges very late. Again these three types form nine combinations of couple. Hence total types of couples on the basis of sexual activities are twenty seven.

In case of the first round of sexual mating done by man, his speed and excitement remains high until the discharge of the seminal fluid and after this, his sexual desire vanishes. When he does the intercourse again, his semen discharges late. The sexual tendency found in ladies is contrary to this. During the first round of sexual intercourse, the sexual feeling of a lady grows gradually and approaches towards the climax but in the second round of mating, her frenzy of love does not remain as strong as was in the first round and also this time her desire does not sustain for a longer duration of time.

आलिङ्गनचुम्बननखच्छेद्यदशनच्छेद्य संवेशनसीत्कृत
पुरुषायितौपरिष्टकानामष्टानामष्टधा विकल्पभेदादष्टा
वष्टकाश्चतुः षष्टिरिति बाभ्रवीयाः ।।
लतावेष्टितकं वृक्षाधिरूढकं तिलतण्डुलकं
क्षीरनीरकमिति चत्वारि सम्प्रयोगकाले ।।
लतेव शालमावेष्टयन्ती चुम्बनार्थं मुखमवनमयेत् । उद्धत्य
मन्दसीत्कृता तमाश्रिता वा किंचिद्रामणीयकं
पश्येत्तल्लतावेष्टितकम् ।।
चरणेन चरणमाक्रम्य द्वितीयेनोरुदेशमाक्रमन्ती वेष्टयन्ती
वा तत्पृष्ठसक्तैकबाहुर्द्वितीयेनांसमवनमयन्ती ईषन्मन्दसीत्कृतकूजिता
चुम्बनार्थमेवाधिरोढुमिच्छेदिति वृक्षाधिरूढकम् ।।
शयनगतावेवोरूव्यत्यासं भुजव्यत्यासं च ससंघर्षमिव धनं
संस्वजेते तत्तिलतण्डुलकम् ।।
रागान्धावनपेक्षितात्ययौ परस्परमनुविशत इवोत्सङ्ग
तायामभि-मुखोपविष्टायां शयने वेति क्षीरजलकम् ।।
शास्त्राणां विषयस्तावद्यावन्मन्दरसा नराः ।
रतिचक्रे प्रवृत्ते तु नैव शास्त्रं न च क्रमः ।।

There are eight steps of normal sexual coalition as hugging or embracing, kissing or smooching, scratching or grazing the partner with nails on being sexually excited or to make sexually excite, biting the partner with teeth in excitement thereby making mark on the body parts, sleeping together or usual sexual coalition, to suck in the breath with a hissing sound showing over excitement, performing *Vipree*

*Rati* or sexual intercourse by making lady lying upon the man and doing the same movement as man do thereby making man still and *Auaprishtik* or oral sex.

There are four kinds of hugging or embracing usually done during sexual intercourse as *Lataveshtitak*, *Vrakshadhirurak*, *Tiltandulak* and *Sheernerak*. Sticking with a man by embracing him like a creeper, bowing own head downwards, keeping the face away from his face and drawing in of the breath in ecstasy by casting a continuous glance over the face of man is *Lataveshtitak*. When a lady embraces a man in such a posture as her one feet lays over the feet of man while another feet is kept on the waist of man thereby she looks like climbing on a tree meantime she keeps her one hand on the back of man and the other on his neck in order to bow it down and tries to ride upon man showing her excitement by producing hissing sound is termed as *Vrakshadhirurak*. When man and woman during the sexual excitement, hold each other tightly with arms and legs while lying on the bed then such hugging is called *Tiltandula*. The strong and deep hugging done by man and woman under the extreme sexual excitement to get into one another is called *Sheernerak*.

It is mentioned in *Kamsutra* that the knowledge of sex is essential for man and woman only till the time they are not sexually excited because the moment they are stimulated,

they show free behavior and at such time they do not depend
upon the rules and regulations pronounced in *Kamsutra*.

रागकाले विशालयन्त्येव जघनं मृगी संविशेदुच्चरते ।।
अवाहसयन्तीव हस्तिनी नीचरते ।।
न्याय्यो यत्र योगस्तत्र समपृष्ठम् ।।
तत्र जघनेन नायकं प्रतिगृह्णीयात् ।।
उत्फुल्लकं विजृम्भितकमिन्द्राणिके चेति त्रितयं मृग्याः प्रायेण ।।
शिरो विनिपात्योर्ध्वं जघनमुत्फुल्लकम् ।।
तत्रापसारं दद्यात् ।।
अनीचे सक्थिनी तिर्यगवसज्य प्रतीच्छेदिति विजृम्भितकम् ।।
उभावप्यूरू ऊर्ध्वाविति तद्द्विग्नकम् ।।
चरणावूर्ध्वं नायकोऽस्या धारयेदिति जृम्भितकम् ।।
तत्कुह्वातावुत्पीडितकम् ।।
तदेकस्मिन्नप्रसारिते ऽर्धपीडितकम् ।।
नायकस्यांस एको द्वितीयकः प्रसारित इति पुनः पुनर्व्यत्यासेन
वेणुदारितकम् ।।
एकः शिरस उपरि गच्छेद्द्वितीयः प्रसारित इति
शूलाचितकमाभ्यासिकम् ।।
संकुचितौ स्वस्तिदेशे निदध्यादिति कार्कटकम् ।।
ऊर्ध्वावूरू व्यत्ययेदिति पीडितकम् ।।
जङ्घाव्यत्यासेन पद्मासनवत् ।।
पृष्ठं परिष्वजमानायाः पराङ् मुखेन परावृत्तकमाभ्यासिकम् ।।
वार्तं तु तत्। शिष्टैरपस्मृतत्वादिति वात्स्यायनः ।।

        In context of the dimensions of the genital organs, if
lady of *Mrigi* type intercourses with a man of *Rishabh* type
then the lady should expand or spread her thighs in order to
broaden the opening of vagina while a lady of *Hastani* type
having deep vagina should keep her thighs near to make the

vaginal path narrow when she intercourses with a man of *Sash* type having small penis. If the couple has comparable dimensioned sexual organs then the lady can keep her thighs in any posture. During the time of sexual intercourse, lady should strongly tie the man with her thighs to achieve more pleasure. As a lady of *Mrigi* type has less depth and small opening of vagina hence she should adopt any of the following three postures during sexual intercourse to make her vaginal path broaden. Those postures are termed as *Utphullak*, *Vijrambhak* and *Indranik*. In case of *Utphullak*, she should lie down and keep some soft item like a pillow below her buttocks or waist to lift up her buttocks. In this method, her head becomes downwards while her hips are up thereby making comfortable man to insert his penis in to her vagina and in this posture she does not feel pain in her over thin and narrow vaginal path. In case of making the posture of *Vijrambhak*, a lady should spread her thighs completely and man should hold them up thereby making perpendicular to her body and insert his penis from any side in a tilted way. When a man holds the spread thighs of woman and keeps her legs in touch of his armpits and then performs the sexual mating then such posture is said to be as *Indranik*.

The great preceptor *Suvarnnabh* describes the postures of sexual mating and says that during the time of mating, if a lady keeps her thighs in touch of each other while holds them up then this kind of posture is termed as *Bhugnak*.

If a man keeps lady's legs on his shoulders to perform mating then this kind of posture is termed as *Jambhitak*. If a lady bents her legs from the knees and puts them below the chest of a man lying upon him for sexual course then such posture is called *Utpidak*. In the same above mentioned posture, if lady keeps her one leg straight lying on the floor while another bent from knees thereby in touch of man's chest and interchanges the positions of both the legs, then such posture is termed as *Ardhpidak*. If a lady keep her legs on the shoulders of the man through the direction of his back hence not letting her legs touching the chest or front part of man who is lying upon him and performing the sexual intercourse then such posture is called *Venudaritak*. When a lady keeps her one leg straight upwards near the head of the man and other leg straight downwards thereby making an angle of almost one hundred and eighty degree angle between the joint of thighs and interchanges the position of both the legs during sexual mating then such posture is termed as *Shulachitak*. A lady who gathers up both the legs like a crab and makes a touch of them with the navel of the man during the sexual mating is said to be in *Karktak* posture. A lady who presses her one thigh tightly by the other thigh and perform sexual course is said to be in *Piditak* posture. A posture of sexual intercourse in which lady folds her legs to make a cross legged posture or make her legs snared at the joints is termed as *Padmasan*. A sex done by the couple in a sitting posture by embracing each other and then changing the position in such a way that man comes on the back side of lady without making penis out of vagina is termed as *Paravrattak* posture. According to *Vatsyayan*, the sexual mating done while roaming or sporting in the water is unethical.

ऊर्ध्वस्थितयोर्यूनोः परस्परापाश्रययोः कुड्यस्तम्भापाश्रितयोर्वा
स्थितरतम् ।।
कुड्यापाश्रितस्य कण्ठावसक्त-बाहुपाशायास्तद्धस्तपञ्जरोपविष्टाया
ऊरूपाशेन जघनमभिवेष्ट्यन्त्या कुड्ये चरणक्रमेण वलन्त्या
अवलम्बितकं रतम् ।।
भूमौ वा चतुष्पदवदास्थितायाः वृषलीलयावस्कन्दनं धेनुकम् ।।
मिश्रीकृतसद्भावाभ्यां द्वाभ्यां सह संघाटकं रतम् ।।
बहीमिश्रश्च सह गोयूथिकम् ।।

According to *Kamasutra*, there are some postures adopted during sexual mating which are normally not brought into play as following:-

When man and woman embrace each other and take the support of a wall or pillar to perform intercourse in standing position is termed as *Isthirrat* posture. When man makes the lady sit on his palms and supports her back through a wall while the lady embraces him by holding at back of his neck and perform sexual mating in a vertical hanging position then this is termed as *Avalambitak* posture. When a lady sits like an animal on the support of her knees and hands while the man performs sexual mating from her back side like an animal is termed as *Dhenuk* posture. If a man sexually intercourse with two ladies simultaneously then such posture is said to be as *Sanghatak*. When a man performs sexual coalition with number of ladies all together then this is called as *Goyuthik*.

स्वाभिप्रायाद्धा विकल्पयोजनार्थिनी ।।

नायककुतूहलाद्धा ।।
तत्र युक्तयन्त्रेणैवेतरेणोत्थप्यामाना तमधः पातयेत् ।
एवं च रतमविच्छिन्नरसं तथा प्रवृत्तमेव स्यात् ।
इत्येकोऽयं मार्गः ।।
पुनरारम्भेणादित एवोपक्रमेत् । इति द्वितीयः ।।
युक्तयन्त्रेणोपसृप्यमाणा यतो दृष्टिमावर्तयेत्तत एवैनां पीडयेत् ।
एतद्रहस्यं युवतीनामिति सुवर्णनाभः ।।
गात्राणां स्रंसनं नेत्रनिमीलनं व्रीडानाशः समधिका च
रतियोजनेति स्त्रीणां भावलक्षणम् ।।
हस्तौ विधुनोति स्विद्यति दशत्युत्थातुं न ददाति पादेनाहन्ति
रतावमाने च पुरुषातिवर्तिनी ।।
तस्याः प्राग्यन्त्रयोगात्करेण संबाधं गज इव क्षोभयेत् ।
आ मृदुभावात् । ततो यन्त्रयोजनम् ।।
न लेवतीं न प्रसूतां न मृगीं न च गर्भिणीम् ।
न चातिव्यायतां नारीं योजयेत्पुरुषायिते ।।

It is said in *Kamsutra* that sometimes ladies with their own will involve themselves into *Vipreet Rati* or reverse way of sexual mating. In this method or posture, lady either lays or sits upon the man who is stable and she inserts his penis in to her vagina thereby doing sexual intercourse by moving up and down in the similar conventional way as a man does. During the time of conventional sexual alliance, when a man lays upon a lady and performs the sexual activity then it is the choice of a lady if she wants to reverse it by coming upon the man without making the penis out from the vagina. If the first round of mating is over and the lady wants to do it again then she should lie upon a man to perform *Vipreet Rati* in order to excite him. According to saint *Suvarnnabh*, a man should press or give massage to only those parts of the body of a lady which excite her more. Ladies possess different level of sensitiveness in different parts of the body. Some ladies get more excitement when their breasts are pressed, some feel more pleasure when their thighs are pressed, some get sexually passionate when their palms are massaged while some get more pleasure when vaginal part or buttocks are pressed. This is the hidden secret to invoke excitement in ladies for sexual mating and a man should first come to know this secret that which body part is more sensitive to touching and pressing of his lady. Following are the symptoms shown by a lady when she gets complete sexual satisfaction: - body parts being loosed, closing her eyes in order to express the satisfaction, diminishing of the feeling of shyness and remain the contact of vagina and penis even after completing the mating. A lady who feels the sexual satisfaction automatically shows such kinds of behavior. After the completion of sexual mating, a lady shows following behavior: - She throws her hands, smeared with sweat and scratches or bits a man with nails or teeth and at this moment the seminal discharger of man takes place. By this time if the lady does not get sexually contented then she remains in the posture of tightly holding the man and does not allow him to stand up thereby leaving her dissatisfied. She even gives up the feeling of shyness by relinquishing the hesitation and tries to carry sexual intercourse by moving her body up and down like a man. If a lady becomes sexually satisfied before his companion then that man should insert a finger into her vagina and should move it here and there inside the vaginal track like an elephant's trunk in order to sexually excite her and the moment vagina gets soaked by the initial discharge, he should insert his penis. A lady who is menstruating, who delivered an infant on the same day, pregnant, who is a *Mrigi* lady or is of less depth of vaginal track and the one with heavy body should not involve themselves in *Vipreet Rati*.

प्रकृत्या मृद्वो रतिप्रिया अशुचिरुचयो निराचाराश्चान्ध्रयः ।।
सकलचतुः षष्टिप्रयोगरागिण्यो ऽश्रीलीलपरूषवाक्यप्रियाः
शयने च सरभसोपक्रमा महाराष्ट्रिका ।।
कुलटाः स्वैरिण्यः परिचारिकाः संवाहिकाश्चाप्येतत् प्रयोजयन्ति ।।
पुरुषाश्च तथा स्त्रीसु कर्मैतत्किल कुर्वते। व्यासम्तस्य च विज्ञेयो
मुखचुम्बनविद्विधिः ।।
परिवर्तितदेहौ तु स्त्रीपुंसौ यत्परस्परम्। युगपत्संप्रयुज्येते स कामः
काकिलः स्मृतः ।।

The lustful ladies who are involved in debauchment are of very soft nature, possess extreme passion for sexual

234

relations, are sexually perverted and are expertise in oral sex. The ladies who are of immoral character and perform adultery are expertise in sexual activities and they sexually excite as well as demoralize men by conversing with extreme verbal vulgarity during sexual coalition.

Almost all eunuchs prefer *Auaprishtik* activity or oral sex. Besides the eunuchs, ladies involved in harlotry, aged ladies seeking young boys for sexual pleasure, stewardess, ladies in the nursing profession and lady servants prefer oral sex hence are often found to be involved in it. Some men prefer making oral sex with ladies. When such a man sucks or kisses the vaginal part of a lady, she feels extreme pleasure. When a man and a woman lies on the bed facing on different sides by putting one's head towards the legs of other's and perform oral sex with each other then it is termed as *Kakil Auaprishtik.*

# <u>Glossary</u>

**Agni Pariksha** : An oath or an obligation performed by one to prove his or her uprightness. This can be done by just putting hand upon fire or *Agni* or by passing through fire.

**Ashtavakra** : *Ashta* means eight and *Vakra* means bend or deformation. Sage *Ashtavakra*'s body was bend from eight parts hence he had a terrible looking appearance. Sage *Uddahalaka* ran a school of spiritual teaching and among his number of pupils, Kahoda was the best. He married his daughter *Sujata* to *Kahoda*. During her pregnancy, *Sujata* regularly joined the spiritual classes of her husband and father. That was highly divine period and the consciousness as well as the perceiving capacity of even a child in womb be very high. Hence the child in womb got well acquainted with the spiritual knowledge. Once in a spiritual speech of *Kahoda* the pronunciation of the Vedic verses done by *Kahoda* go incorrect and the child in the womb instructed the right pronunciation thereby interrupting in-between the speech. When this happened eighth times, *Kahoda* got furious and cursed his own son in the womb to suffer from eight abnormalities. Therefore the baby born with eight curves in the form of deformities in his body and hence named *Ashtavakra*.

**Brahama** : The God of creation as per Hindu mysticism, also known as *Prajapati*. The destiny of human being as well as a of the creatures is decided by *Brahama* and no other deity or power can change it. At the beginning of the creation, Lord *Brahama* created eleven *Prajapatis* named as *Marici, Atri, Angiras, Pulastya, Pulaha, Kratuj, Vashishtha, Daksha, Bhrigu* and *Narada*. These creations of *Brahama* are said to be his *Manas Putra* or the progenies who took birth because of spiritual coalition or without physical union. The Lord *Brahama* is self born through a lotus flower which grew from the navel of Vishnu. He is traditionally depicted with four heads and four arms to look and control over the earth in all the four directions. His age is said to be of thirty one million ten thousand and four hundred crores solar years also termed as 100 *Brahama* years. His vehicle is a glorious swan.

**Dharamshastra** : Religious scriptures.

**Draupadi** : An adopted daughter of king *Drupad* of *Panchaal*. She became the wife of five *Pandavas* and at the end of the battle of *Mahabharatha*, she became the queen of *Hastinapur*. She was born from the sacrificial fire of *Yagya*, performed by *Drupad*. As she was made from consecrated fire, her body was formed directly from one of the content *Pawak* or *Agni* or fire of *Panch Tatwa* that is "*Kshiti-Jal-Pawak-Gagan-Samira*". Hence she was destined to marry with five men, one as her husband and rest four to accomplish the remaining part of *Panch Tatwa*. This happened to her as her father set up a *Swayambar* for her and declared that who ever wants *Draupadi* as his wife had to shoot the eye of a fish stick at a revolving target while looking only at it's reflection in a bowl. Arjuna successfully tackled the target while other princes were unable to accomplish it. As Pandavas were on exile hence they were earning their living by begging. Their mother Kunti advised them to share every thing equally they get by begging. When Arjuna came back with his newly wife Draupadi, all brothers were happy to see it and asked mother to come out from the cottage to see what they brought. As usual, mother said them to share equally what ever they had brought. Then all the five brothers married her. She is often sexually blamed by the followers of pseudo religions for being the wife of five husbands who are unknown to the facts behind this. She is also sometimes blamed by few sexually corrupt and morally perverted Hindus.

**Ganga** : A river of Indian subcontinent rising in the Himalayan mountains and flowing around 2600 kilometers through a vast plain region to the bay of Bengal. River Ganga is revered as a goddess whose purity cleanses the sins of all the creatures whoever takes a bath in that. It is believed that drinking the water of river Ganga provides physical as well as mental purity.

**Gita** : One of the most sacred scripture of Hinduism comprising 700 verses. It is a part of Mahabharata comprising eighteen chapters from twenty fifth to forty two. The content of Gita is the conversation between lord Krishna and Arjuna taking place on the battlefield before the starting of great war of *Mahabharata*. In this, responding to *Arjun*'s confusion and moral dilemma about fighting his own relatives, lord *Krishna* explains him his duties and the actuality of the life.

**Kamdeva** : The God of love and sensual pleasure. He is a young man who wields bow and arrows made of sugarcane. *Kamdeva* married his consort *Rati*, the deity of sexual union. He shoots with his bow, the five flower tipped shafts of desire. He is the son of goddess *Lakshmi* and *Vishnu*. As the lord *Brahama* is considered to be the originator of earth and all the creatures hence because *Kamdeva* is responsible for sexual passion and coalition thereby being the cause of new incoming generations, said to be the son of lord *Brahama*.

**Kanyadaan/Saptapadi** : *Kanyadaan* is a very significant ritual performed by the father of the bride at the time of marriage. The father pours out sacred water as a symbol of giving away his daughter to the bridegroom. In this the right hand of the bride is placed over the right hand of the groom and a promise is given by bridegroom to take care of the bride in whole of the life. In *Saptapadi*, seven encirclements of the consecrated fire are taken by the couple. During this, either the corner of the garments of couple is tied together or the groom holds the bride's right hand in his own right hand. Every such round around the sanctified fire is affiliated to a specific oath.

**Karma** : Duties or obligations.

**Kritya** : A powerful female deity, capable to perform any kind of incantation. There are sixty-four *Krityas* affiliated to different requirements. They are considered to be powerful weapon to destroy the enemies and to protect one from any type of black magic.

**Lord Krishna :** The eighth human form of God *Vishnu*. He appeared on the midnight of the eighth day of the dark half of the month of *Sravana* on July 19th 3228 BC. He exhibited his human appearance for a little over 125 years and disappeared on February 18th 3102 BC on the new moon night of *Phalguna*. His departure marks the beginning of the current age of dishonesty known as *Kaliyug*.

**Moksha :** This is also termed as *Mukti*, means liberation from the cycle of rebirth or reincarnations and true realization of God. It is assumed that the rebirth of any living species may take place in any of eighty four millions forms of creatures including human being. This rebirth of a human being on the earth depends on the virtuous and awful deeds performed by him in his life span. A man has to suffer grief in the hell after death for his awful deeds and when such punishment is over he is send to the earth in the form of different creatures to which he misbehaved in his past human life. A person, who follows the virtuous way of life, never commits even a peccadillo or any kind of sin, never speaks or performs ill of others and considers all human beings as well as creatures to be equivalent, achieves *Moksha* thereby gets rid of the grief of hell as well as rebirth.

**Mundan/ Mundan Sanskar** : The first haircut of baby. *Sanskar* means the traditional ritual followed by Hindu families. This *Mundan Sanskar* is done either in the first year or the third year of the age. A priest is called to conduct the rituals and a barber is called to shave off the hair. This is one of the sixteen *Sanskar*s followed by Hindus. The sixteen *Sanskar* are as follows: *Garbhadhan*: Conception, *Punsavana*: Fetus protection, *Simanta*: Blessing to pregnant Mother, performed in the fourth month of pregnancy, *Jaat-Karmaa*: Child Birth celebration normally performed on sixth day or after eleventh day, *Naamkarna*: Naming Child, *Nishkramana*: Taking the child outdoors usually performed on or after forty days, *Annaprashan*: Giving the child solid food performed after six months when teeth develops first, *Mundan* or *Choula*: Hair cutting, *Karnavedh*: Ear piercing, *Yagyopraveet*: Providing sacred thread to child. It indicates that the child can perform any rituals should be performed at the early age of life but usually performed before marriage, *Vedarambh*: Study of Vedas and Scriptures, *Samaavartana*: Completing education, *Vivaah*: Marriage, *Sarvasanskar*: Preparing for Renouncing, *Sanyas*: Renouncing the world thereby being ascetic *Antyeshti* or *Aurdhadwrahik* Karma: Last rite or funeral rites.

**Namuchi** : *Namuchi* was a brawny demon who subjugated lord *Indra* in a battle and detained him. He allowed letting *Indra* go on assurance as a boon not to slay him by day or by night with any weapon wet or dry. *Indra* promised him and was set free by him. In time, lord *Indra* cut his head at twilight the duration in between day and night and by water foam which was neither wet nor dry.

**Narad** : Sage *Narad* was a traveling monk with multiple personality having the capability to visit distant planets by flying. He is considered to be a divine messenger of god, a renowned teacher and a notorious mischief maker. He is considered to be the *Manas Putra* or the progeny born by the thoughts of lord *Brahama*. He is also famous as a mischief maker and a quarrel monger and in India, a person delights in back biting, spreading rumors and gossiping is symbolically chided as *Narad*.

**Navratri** : *Nav* means nine and *Ratri* means nights. This is the most holy festival of Hindus. This festival is commenced on the first day of the bright fortnight of the lunar month. In this fasting of nine days and worshipping mother goddess in her different forms is done.

**Panch Mahabhuta/Panch Tatwa** : It is considered and even found true that all matters in the universe comprised of five elements, termed as *Panch Tatwa*. These elements include of *Apo* or *Jal* or water, *Thejo* or *Pawak* or fire, *Vayu* or *Samira* or air, *Prithivi* or *Kshiti* or earth and *Akash* or *Gagan* or sky. *Panch Mahabhuta* are the deities associated with these five elements.

**Pandava/Udhishthir/Arjun** : *Pandavs* were five son of king *Pandu* by his two wives *Kunti* and *Madri*. There names were

242

*Udhishthir, Bheem, Arjun, Nakul* and *Sahedev*. All the brothers were married with the same woman *Draupadi*. The *Pandavas* had the battle with their other brothers in the field of *Kurukshetra* in which Lord Krishna drive the charioteer of *Arjun*.

**Puran** : These are the religious texts consisting of the narratives of the history of the universe from creation to destruction, genealogies of the kings and the demigods as well as the descriptions of the Hindu cosmology, philosophy and geography. The almost description done is in the form of true stories. These are eighteen in count and are as follows: *Brahama Puran, Padma Puran*(In seven parts as *Sristhi Khand, Bhumi Khand, Swarga Khand, Brahama khand, Patala Khand, Uttara Khand* and *Kriya Khand*), *Vishnu Puran, Shiv Puran, Bhagwat Puran, Narad Puran*(In two parts as *Purva Bhag* and *Uttara Bhag*), *Markandeya Puran, Agni Puran, Bhavishya Puran, Brahama Vaivart Puran, Varaha Puran, Linga Puran, Skanda Puran, Vaman Puran, Matsya Puran, Garun Puran, Vayu Puran* and *Kurma Puran*.

**Rudra** : A *Rigvedic* God of storm and devastation, considered to be an earlier form of lord *Shiva*. Often used as a synonym of lord *Shiva*. It literally indicates to one with terrible persona, whose roar even is sufficient to flow fear in the bones of enemies and evils.

**Sari** : This is an Indian female garment in the form of strip of unstitched cloth ranging from four to nine meters in length.

Ladies wrap this around the waist with one end and ther drape it over the shoulder baring the midriff.

**Smriti/Manu Smriti** : These are the principal code of socia law taken from the essence of Vedas. *Smritis* stands next ir authority to Vedas and it provides the codes of conduct a well as laws to regulate Hindu society. The eighteen *Smriti* are named on their creator's name and are termed as *Man Smriti, Parasar Smriti, Yagyavalkya Smriti, Gautam Smriti Harita Smriti , Yam Smriti , Vishnu Smriti, Sankha Smrit Likhita Smriti, Brahaspati Smriti, Daksha Smriti, Angira Smriti, Pracetas Smriti, Samvarta Smriti, Acanas Smriti, At. Smriti, Apastamba Smriti* and *Satatapa Smriti*.

**Sukracharaya/Devayani/Kach** : *Sukracharaya* was the gran son of great sage *Bhrigu*. He was the Guru of demons an was familiar with the *Sanjeevani Vidya* or the art of makin dead alive. As the demons were more powerful than mer hence they often fight with deities to occupy the paradise an in every such battle, *Sukracharaya* make alive every devi who demised. Unfortunately deities were not familiar with thi art hence every time they fight with devils, they loose the wa Ultimately the guru of deities, lord *Brahaspati*, sent his so *Kach* to *Sukracharaya* to learn that magical *Sanjeevani Vidya Kach* lived with *Sukracharaya* long time as his pupil. Th daughter of *Sukracharaya, Devayani* fell in love with *Kach*. A the demons were familiar with this fact that *Kach* was the so of *Brahaspati* and he was there to know about the art c

244

making dead alive. They all were worried that through the *Kach*, deities might get the utter spiritual art hence once when *Kach* was in the forest to get wood for the sacrificial act of Guru, they cut him in pieces and burned him. When Kach did not come back till late night, *Devayani*, who was in love with him, requested her father to find him out. *Sukracharaya* came to know that his pupil was dead. *Devayani* was very beloved to her father *Sukracharaya* and she insisted her father to make *Kach* alive. *Sukracharaya* chanted the *versses* of the magical art of *Sanjeevani* and *Kach* got alive. The demons got worried to see this but they were unable to compel their Guru *Sukracharaya* hence next time they cut the body of *Kach* and burned it to ashes, mixed in a beverage and fed to *Sukracharaya*. Again when *Kach* was not back till late evening, *Devayani*, insisted her father to search for him. This time when *Sukracharaya* chanted the verses to make *Kach* alive, his voice came inside his stomach. *Sukracharaya* knew that if he made *Kach* alive then he would come out of his stomach by tearing it hence first he taught the art of making alive to *Kach* then made him alive. He came out by tearing the stomach of *Sukracharaya* and then he made alive his Guru by the spiritual verses.

**Vajapeya Yagya** : *Vaja* means rice or grain and *peya* means a beverage. Hence *Vajapeya Yagya* or *Vajapeya* sacrifice is done to bring the affluence in grains and water. At the famine period, this kind of sacrifice brings remedy to adverse situation and enhances crops as well as the natural sources of water. The authentic person performing this sacrifice is bathed by rice, poured over him as water, hence this sacrifice is termed as *Vajapeya*. This sacrifice consists of the *Ahuti* of *Soma Rasa*, twenty three *pasu* or animals and *Vaja* or rice.

**Vedic/Veda** : Veda are the ancient most sacred texts of Indo Aryans. They are now proved to be the first spiritual religious books among the any existing religious scripture of any religion. There are four Vedas as follows:

*RigVeda*: The oldest scripture containing 10600 verses and 1028 Sanskrit hymns recited by ultimate intellectual priests.

*YajurVeda*: It consists of archaic prose verses. Sectioned in two areas termed as Black *YajurVeda* or Krishna *YajurVeda* and white *YajurVeda* or *Shukla YajurVeda*.

*Samaveda*: It consists of One thousand five hundreds and forty nine stanza taken almost entirely from *RigVeda*.

*AtharvaVeda*: Consist of 760 hymns. Most of the verses are metrical but few sections are in prose. It's initial part consist of incantations concerned with protection against demons and disaster. The later part consists of texts with speculative and philosophical hymns.

**Vishnu/Mahesh** : Vishnu is worshipped as a God of nourishment and life. Twenty two incarnations of Vishnu took place on the earth in which Lord *Ram* and Lord *Krishna* are well known. *Chatanaya Mahaprabhu* were twenty fourth incarnation and *Ramkrishna Paramhansa*(1836-1886), even after being a great worshipper of Goddess *kali*, were twenty fifth incarnation.

**Yagya** : A *Vedic* ritual of sacrifice, performed to gratify the deities. In this, the oblations are poured into sacrificial fire termed as divine *Agni* with the belief that all the offered items directly reaches to the specific God. Such offering of different items into the sacred fire is termed as *Ahuti*. There is appointed a main priest along with number of other priest to perform *Ahuti*. Vedic verses are chanted together in a proper way by the priests sitting around the fire and *Ahuti* is performed with the name of different Gods. Such every step of *Ahuti* is directly bestowed upon the God whose name is chanted along with.

**Yaksha** : They are the tutelary Gods of forests and villages often viewed as the steward deities of the earth and the wealth buried beneath. They are considered to be the caretakers of the natural treasures hidden in the earth. They have dual personality as on the one hand they may be inoffensive fairy ready to help impoverished people while on other hand they may be a kind of cannibalistic monster, ghost or demon.

**Yoni** : When used in context of women's genital organs, it indicates to vagina. In broad sense, it indicates to different incarnations taken by creatures or different forms of human or animals obtained by rebirth.

**Yug/Yuga** : It literally means long period or an era. As per the Hindu methodology, the life on earth is divided in four main parts comprising of numerous secondary parts. The basic four parts are *Sat Yug, Treta Yug, Dwapar Yug* and *Kali Yug*.

*Sat Yug* : It lasts for 1,728,000 years. Life span of human was of 100,000 years. Lord *Vishnu* incarnated in four forms as *Matsya, Kurma,Varaha* and *Narsimha*.

*Treta Yug* : it lasts for 1,296,000 years and the average life span of the people was of 10,000 years. Lord *Vishnu* incarnated in the form of *Vamana, Parashuram* and lord *Ram*.

*Dwapar Yug* : It lasts for 864,000 years and the average life span of human being was of 1000 years. *Vishnu* incarnated in the form of Lord *Krishna* in this era.

*Kali Yug* : This is the present era of the expected period of 432,000 years and the average life span of human being is 100 years. *Vishnu* incarnated in the form of *Buddha* while the next incarnation of *Vishnu* in this era is supposed to be *Kalki* who will be responsible for the great devastation on the earth thereby making the end of all of the creatures including human.

# From The Author

It is very arduous to write something factual on women in the contemporary scenario because the authors, poets and media had expressed so much ambiguous and deceptive particulars in the human society that now it has been difficult to shallow the curtain of delusion by expressing the bare truth of women. The outcome of the exceptionally deep studies and surveys done regarding women was almost against of the opinion of the society and it was so awful that it would be a betrayal to humanity if the truth found are not kept in the knowledge of the society. It is not very easy to express real thoughts on any subject in the present scenario even after having freedom to verbalize and women is a such blazing subject on which if one expresses the untruth by decorating with poetic view, morphology, phraseology and high-flown language thereby presents the women's sexual aspect, helplessness and harassments then it will be injustice to the Goddess of justice while if the naked truth of women is expressed by not effected from their body charm then what will happen is needless to state here.

It is fortunate and a subject of proud for one to take birth in the pious land of Indian subcontinent. The honor of the goddess is provided to women by the soil of this country. If women are really respected in any part of the earth then that is India. What was the outcome of this honor and reverence that was given to women from the very ancient period and up to which extent women could maintain their dignity that is expressed in next section of the book "Women, The Actuality".

Unfortunately in the present scenario while comparing the iniquitous and moral attributes in men and women, the assessment of men is done by judging the attitudes of immoral men who are of twenty percent of the overall population of men while the assessment of women is done by judging the disposition of morally high and innocent women who are less than eighth percent of the overall populace of women. Hence it is considered that men are the symbol of wrongdoings and the women are the symbol of fairness, mercy and morality while the actual situation is just reverse of it. Indian judiciary and administration is almost biased and it can be easily seen in the rules and regulations as well as in the decisions that have been taken in the past in favor of women by disregarding the rights of innocent men. This unfairness of harassing the innocent men by helping the corrupt women is stimulated by human rights and numerous women organizations.

The forthcoming book "Women, The Actuality" is not only regarding the modern ladies of the Indian subcontinent instead that is a mirror to the exposed and concealed veracity beneath the thoughts, speech and performances of women residing in any part of the earth. I am quite sure that no lady will be able to conceal her actual appearance from this mirror even if she extensively decorates herself artificially and she will get her concrete illustration in this mirror, perhaps in the form of the most disgusting reflection of society.

# About The Author

Ashok Kumar Pant born in Mumbai, a metro city of Indian subcontinent, in 1972 and is presently residing in Lucknow. Professionally being a software engineer, he started his journey of literature from "It Is Continued". He devoted himself in writing on the subjects like women psychology, moral degradation of the society and unbinding sexual corruptions. The bitter practical experiences of Indian society and unavoidable arousing emotions compelled him to write as an attempt to save the humanity.